TRAVELS
IN
TRANSOXIANA

TRAVELS
IN
TRANSOXIANA

In Lands over the Hindu-Kush and Across the Amu Darya

Jaswant Singh

Rupa & Co

Copyright © Jaswant Singh 2006

Published 2006 by

Rupa & Co

7/16, Ansari Road, Daryaganj,
New Delhi 110 002

Sales Centres:

Allahabad Bangalore Chandigarh Chennai
Hyderabad Jaipur Kathmandu
Kolkata Mumbai Pune

Typeset in 11 pts. Revival by
Nikita Overseas Pvt. Ltd.
1410 Chiranjiv Tower
43 Nehru Place
New Delhi 110 019

Printed in India by
Gopsons Papers Ltd.
A-2 & 3, Sector-64
Noida 201 301

To the eternal traveler: forever moving, forever searching

" 'Is there anybody there?' Said the Traveller,
Knocking on the moonlit door;
And his horse in the silence champed the grasses
of the forest's ferny floor."

'The listeners'–1912,
Walter de la Mare

Contents

Acknowledgements

Peter Levi in *The Frontiers of Paradise* cites what he found inscripted in a well-shaft of a monastic cloister "O sobria ebrietas, O ebria sobrietas": 'O sober drunkenness, O drunken sobriety'. Though describing a state of fervour born of ascetic ardour and deep meditation, this yearning for travel, what the Germans call wanderlust, is not too far removed from "sober drunkenness". I acknowledge unreservedly, therefore, this first debt. The very first gratitude is to that spirit of travel which has impelled me—all my life.

Otherwise, of course, this book would not be here at all.

My thanks to Garima Saxena for her professional skill in designing the cover of the book with a sense of detail, though the photographs (on the cover and within) are the result of my amateur snap shot taking.

My appreciation to Ashwini Channan and his team consisting of Natarajan Swaminathan, Anjan Bhowmick, Kashi Ram, Vikas Thotada for giving the book its final shape.

And then my special thanks to Sanjana Roy Choudhury for her sure and professional editing and the entire team at Rupa & Co. for their valuable contribution in bringing this publication to the stands.

I must acknowledge a debt to Robert Byron's *The Road to Oxiana* too, from which I got the inspirations of *Travels in Transoxiana: In Lands over the Hindu-Kush and Across the Amu Darya.*

Before The Beginning

SOME JOURNEYS BEGIN WELL BEFORE THEY ACTUALLY DO, THIS certainly did for in my mind I had set off on my travels well before any 'first step' had been taken.

The seed, or rather the 'seeds', of my 'Travels in Transoxiana' were sown long back. They had then lain dormant awaiting the catalyst, just that correct chemistry of time, resource and circumstances to come together. And when I set off—I also wondered—what would that be like? How was I then to write about it? I longed of course to be able to do so say like Norman Lewis, that bewitching ability to instantly capture a mood, an ambience, a place in just a few sentences—a few masterly flicks of the paint brush. Witness his arrival in Rangoon: 'it spreads as a dark stain into the midnight sea. Soon the inert grey of water lifted to the horizon, the darkness... followed.... sprinkled with points of light. There was a blurred reflection... of the wasting moon; the blinking of lamps strung out in lines, leading web-like to the centre of some unseen city...'[1] Magical, but then few have written travelogues like Norman

---

1. *Golden Earth: Travels in Burma* by Norman Lewis; p.13; pub. ELAND, 1952.

Lewis, or have his great ability to see, to catch the essence and then to be able to say so much in such little space:...'for Mingaladon Airport it could at least be said that it did not suffer from the cosmopolitan insipidity natural to airports'. Patrick Leigh Fermor was an adolescent, ran into serious problems at school, therefore, opted to journey on foot from London to Constantinople: 'I got out of bed on the great day, put on my new kit and tramped South-West under a lowering sky... Shepherd's market was prickly with falling drops'. From that journey were born *A Time of Gifts*: *Between the Woods and the Water*[2], unmatched travel accounts. Uniquely so also Robert Byron in that great travel classic: *The Road to Oxiana*[3]. It opens beguilingly: 'Venice, 20 August 1933, Here as a joy hog: a pleasant change after that mission on the Giudecca[4] two years ago'................and then, just a few sentences later apropos really of nothing..... 'after a paddle in the sea, Bertie mentioned that all 'whales' have syphilis'.

Travel of course is an adventure, but it is also an escape, a getting away, so much of a search too, which in the guise of a place to visit or a destination to reach is often a search, for the 'self'! Invariably then there is great romance in travel. Leigh Fermor was asked by his mother what he wanted for the journey: 'The other half of my very conventional traveling library', he recounts, 'was the Loeb Horace, Vol. 1 which my mother had bought', on the fly leaf of which she had written 'The translation of a short poem by Petronius, chanced on and copied out, she told me later, from another volume on the same shelf':

---

2. *A Time of Gifts*: *Between the Woods and the Water* by Patrick Leigh Fermor; p. 15; pub John Murray, UK, 1977.
3. *The Road to Oxiana* by Robert Byron—This title has inspired me to entitle my efforts as *Travels in Transoxiana*.
4. Giudecca: An island off the Venice Coast where that great and stylish hotel 'Cipriani' is.

'Leave thy home, O youth! and seek out alien shores....
Yield not to misfortune:
the far off Danube shall know thee...'[5]

Mystics, wanderers, monks and pilgrims always travel—have
always done so through the centuries: constantly seeking, searching,
at times for a holy site, often for salvation of the self, mostly though,
and so much more modestly, for just plain virtue. Since travelling
monks and priests always have more to 'give' than to receive, they
travel therefore as 'traders of faith', as evangelists to propound their
belief as the final, the only and the ultimate Truth. Peter Levi, in
elegant sentences of limpid clarity, informs in *The Frontiers of
Paradise: A Study of Monks and Monasteries*[6] that 'early Indian
mendicant monks were the first of all.... who met in certain caves
to shelter (during) the rainy season. These caves became their
monastery and their home.... vast assemblies of Buddhist monks in
Afghanistan, at places like the refuge valley of Bamyan....
honeycombed with caves, (give) a sense of missionary pilgrimage...
It was the monks who carried Buddhism to China along the silk
roads, and Chinese Buddhist monks on pilgrimage to the home
shrines provide our best records of what Buddhist Afghanistan was
once like'.[7] That is why the existence of shrines and pilgrimage to
them are so 'closely intertwined', and in all faiths.

Travellers there have always been, through centuries, and
explorers too, who sought new lands, charted new courses, went to
far-off, unknown, untrod upon places; mountaineers and sea farers,
the adventurous, always thirsting for the unknown, the exotic, the
different, the 'unconquered'. It was a certain spirit that always

5. *A Time of Gifts: Between the Woods and Water* by Patrick Leigh Fermor; p.
   15; pub John Murray, UK, 1977
6. *The Frontiers of Paradise: A Study of Monks and Monasteries* by Peter Levi;
   p. 40; pub. Collins Harvill, UK, 1987.
7. ibid.

moved outwards, but then it is also a certain 'type' who alone set out, who travel. These few, restless spirits who sought then, or seek now, are not a mass product; restlessly they seek as nature's true gypsies, 'wandering spirits' at peace with themselves only when afoot; an immense sense of peace, a great liberation, a freedom then settles upon them, but only then. Almost all the writings of Wilfred Thesiger—that great traveller and unbound spirit—echoes this thought whenever he sets out. He crossed that truly impossible of all deserts: 'The Rab-al-khali,' (The Empty Quarter) on foot. Not content with just one crossing, he did it a second time, recounting these journeys memorably in *Arabian Sands*[8]. Or take the epic crossing of the polar wastes—the heroism of Scott and his companions—and so many countless others. All of them sought to quench, to give expression, as all travellers do to some unquenched yearning. Which is why so much of travel writing is autobiographical. Otherwise it would be no more than just a brochure of visits.

In the twentieth century, as the world shrank and our planet had fewer and fewer places left that had not, till then, been set foot upon, travelling became increasingly prosaic, it lost the thrill of discovering the unknown. Wildernesses got tamed; they no longer had the splendour of solitude. The menace of mass tourism had arrived. The aeroplane and the automobile robbed travellers of challenge, the sweat of physical hardship, long, arduous journeys on foot, in the saddle, or the fatiguing tedium of a camel's back. It is interesting why so often travel writing is accompanied by scholarship and is yet a search and a yearning for it; also aestheticism—subjective and individual, of course, but invariably present as an attribute. And then a kind of asceticism: unstated, unacknowledged, perhaps even unknown to the traveller but always there, always in this act of shedding the worldly, a giving up even if temporarily of the comforts of the familiar. Also because travel so often also uniquely offers an

---

8. *Arabian Sands* by Wilfred Thesiger; pub. William Collins Sons and Co. Ltd., 1959.

innate sense of the spiritual and obviously romance and eroticism, too. The hippies, as a cult of the sixties sought the new and the erotic, yes, but along with that ever present was this thirst to find answers to the hollowness of the spirit of our times.

I was born in a land, and in a period which have vanished, having been compressed unnaturally in space and time by circumstance, by the assault of that unrelenting invader—'the new'. This 'land' got 'lost' because it was bewildered by this attack of the 'new'; we were totally uncomprehending of the challenge of those times and had no adequate response to it. In the process, we became so much poorer—ethically, culturally and emotionally. I rue greatly, and almost every day, that an entire way of life—our way—in that glorious desert of our country just went away, vanished... forever.

It is impossible to communicate adequately the magical pull of the desert—'empty wastes...a desiccated land which knows nothing of gentleness or ease ...', yet men have lived here since the dawn of time, their faint footprints and 'fire blackened stones of cooking fires', and headstones commemorating valiant heroes of old dot our sands. I have, from my childhood witnessed—indeed experienced— the near total transformation of the central ethos of this 'cruel land which casts a spell such as none other can'. I grew up when, at least to us, even a box of matches was a rarity, and fire was still often lit by flint and stone and some fluffy stuff that would burn but only after much persuasion. As a wonder struck infant I often sat and watched riveted, the sparks as the flint struck against the stone— again and again, until finally a spark smouldered that fluff; then followed the slow, gentle, patient blowing and nursing and tending, coaxing almost—until suddenly a small tongue of flame leapt bravely up. This is perhaps why we were taught as children to never extinguish fire by throwing water over it, to always cover it and that too, preferably, by ash. But I have wandered too far, because this 'going back' in memory is altogether a different journey.

What influences or factors shaped me into a kind of a restless seeker, I cannot determine. Travel had always drawn me irresistibly, the thought of it, dreams of it, the planning—maps and pictures and accounts of distant places and peoples—cluttered my mind and my tables even as a school boy. Very early I had sensed, not through any form of learning process, but rather as an instinctive cognition that history is shaped, influenced, almost determined, by the geography of our living space. Then our folklore and folk sayings, our myths and traditions, our living history—all greatly influenced me. There was so much to think about, so much had changed, so much was changing. Why? Who is changing it? How? But then so often our queries, our concerns, our worries can be answered only by ourselves, not by any other. Precocious and indiscriminate in my early reading, the romance of Iran and Afghanistan and Balkh and Bokhara and names like Uzbek and Turkmen and Khorasan, also Central Asia, drew me irresistibly, as iron fillings are drawn to a magnet. Tradition, chance and circumstances then made me volunteer for the Army. I was commissioned when barely nineteen, as an officer in The Central India Horses, in that golden period of 'cantonment soldiering' in the Indian Army. Our independence after all was but ten years old. Almost immediately thereafter, I began to volunteer for every possible deep reconnaissance in the Himalayas, as they were then being ordered frequently, even if these missions were not always accompanied by any easily discernible plan or design. Snow clothing or advanced equipment were undreamt of, it was odd to even ask. But this is again an impermissible traverse in memory.

Babur, his personality, his exploits and his writing fascinated me greatly.[9] Though I had no historical basis I did always hear at home that when Rana Sanga confronted Babur in Khanwa, an ancestor of ours with his band of horsemen had also joined the great Rana to confront the invader. Of Akbar I did not, simply could not share the praise, the near adulation that history books and discourse outside of my home surroundings invariably showered. The reasons were and remain entirely subjective.

---

9. See 'A note on Babur', p. 15.

BEFORE THE BEGINNING | 7

Should you ever chance to visit that ancient and venerated fort of Chittorgarh, where every stone in its ramparts has a tale of great heroism and sacrifice to tell, then as you go up the winding 'ghati' (climb) of it, tarry a while after the main and imposing 'Pol'-Gate, there, on the right, are two cenotaphs—one commemorates Jaimalji, the other Kalloji. They were both killed in the third great 'saka', (very inadequately and prolonged and bloodly seige) of Chittor. This great destruction was Akbar's doing in AD 1568. Read about it if it interests you. It is medieval history, yes, but it is an account of stirring valour and great chivalry by these two. Kalloji was my ancestor; he had travelled from our desert vastnesses with his small band to volunteer his services in defense of Chittor against Akbar the invader. The rest followed. Now, every Sunday, at his cenotaph a fair assembles—regularly, without fail. He is still worshipped. The devotees believe that 'He' cures ailments. They present 'Him' offerings of liquor too. Myth has it that he can occasionally still be sighted; and not because of the liquor: a giant, sword wielding figure slaying 'the alien invaders of Chittor, protecting the poor and curing the ill'. There is, alas, no similar cenotaph to Akbar here and also no such myth; he is not worshipped either, to my knowledge, not anywhere in Mewar or Marwar.

But about Babur I always held an altogether different view. Who was this Babur? What brought him here? From where did he arrive to alter the course of our history? And in this manner was planted the first seed of *Travels in Transoxiana*. It lay germinating for very long. Perhaps, for a similar reason this travelogue, too, has taken so long to bear fruit.

But the 'search', in reality goes way beyond all this. These ancient lands that lie beyond the Amu Darya—or what the Greeks around 300 BC named as the Oxus are, and have always been to me, the 'crucible of mankind'. From these lands have emerged, time and again not just Babur but so many other more formidable forces of primeval energy, sweeping aside all that then faced them.

Millennium after millennium, as centuries receded in time, these irresistible 'forces of change': 'Sakas' (Scythian to the Greeks), Huns,

Mongols emerged, one after another, to conquer all. In Transbaikalia, in the cold fastnesses of the steppes of Mongolia was born a fierce warrior: hard, unrelenting, uncaring and unstoppable, like the mighty river of time itself; he conquered all that came in his way. His name—Changez. It is from these origins that then emerged the great Turkic—Mongol Empire. These were truly the early 'clashes of civilisations'; and they have always occurred, through time, whenever a new thought has emerged to challenge the existing. It is here, and in consequence that was also born this conflict between Christianity and Islam. Though, Islam came here much later, subscription to it was, at first, just a 'thin layer of superficial observances', upon the much older and stronger sub-stratum of ancestor worship, of animistic beliefs, also similar other convictions and superstitions. Bernard Lewis with eloquent erudition comments in *What Went Wrong*[10] 'Islam...... created a world civilization, polyethnic, multiracial, international.....' It 'represented the greatest military power on earth—its armies, at the very same time were invading Europe and Africa, India and China'. It was the 'foremost economic power' of its time, in the world, 'importing slaves and gold', (and wool) from Africa, from Europe, and exchanging a variety of goods and manufactures with the 'civilized countries of Asia'. It had achieved the highest level so far in human history in the arts and sciences of civilisation. Inheriting the knowledge and skills of the ancient Middle East, of Greece and of Persia, China and from India... It was in the Islamic Middle East that 'Indian numbers were for the first time incorporated in the inherited body of mathematical learning....then transmitted to the West, where they are now called Arabic numerals, honoring not those who invented them in India but those who first brought them to Europe'. For 'medieval Muslims, Christendom was the Byzantine Empire', the 'remoter lands of Europe' being just 'outer darkness of barbarism', worthy only of slave trade and no more.

---

10. *What Went Wrong* by Bernard Lewis; pp.6-7 and 8; pub. Weidenfeld & Nicolson Great Britain, 2002.

But in this unrelenting grind of centuries, all eventually turns to dust, the tide always turns; 'the relationship changed', Islam was forced back. Those that had knocked on 'Christendom's gates at Vienna' failed, in 1683, in their second siege. Ottoman chronicler Silihdar, quoted by Lewis observed: 'This was a calamitous defeat, so great that there has never been its like since the first appearance of the Ottoman state.' Earlier, for Christendom, the 'final defeat of the Moors in Spain, in 1492, and the liberation of Russia from the rule of the Islamised Tatars were seen as decisive victories. Like the Spaniards and Portuguese, the Russians' (who had earlier been conquered by the Tartar Golden Horde and made subjects to Muslims) 'pursued their former masters into their homelands ....reaching (in 1554) the shores of the Caspian Sea' then, 'the northern shore of the Black Sea, thus, beginning the long process of conquest and colonization that incorporated vast Muslim lands in the Russian Empire'. Bernard Lewis quotes that the Turks lamented their loss thus:

'In the fountains they no longer play
In the mosques they no longer pray
The places that prospered are now desolate
The Austrian has taken our beautiful Buda.'

But we have again come too far forward, travelled too fast, skipped too many centuries. Well before Islam, several other thoughts, other influences and forces had reached these lands. The great and illuminating thoughts of Buddha, for one. But even before Buddha, 'it is established that cultural and trading relations between Central Asia and the Indian subcontinent in the third and second millenniums BC were closer than they are described by many contemporary researchers'.[11] As for Central Asia, this period is often described as the period of the emergence in these lands of

---

11. *India and Central Asia (Pre-Islamic period)* by T. Shirinov, pp.10, 11, 14.

Buddha's tranquil visage, his message of the 'Eight fold path', of brotherhood and compassion and peace. Trade routes, that brought the faith here, (along of course with Monks) developed, and there were several such routes—one for example, from the 'Punj valley to the territories of present day Tajikistan, Uzbekistan, North Afghanistan and South Turkmenistan'.[12] It is also now 'established that the agricultural population of Central Asia had cultural relations with the Indus civilization via trading stations'[13] ....also, 'cowry shells from the Indian Ocean....... have been found in 'large quantities in different Central Asian settlements of the Bronze and Early iron Age',[14] yet again as evidence of long-distance trading relations. Merchants and missionaries were the first to carry Buddhism to the Central Asian region. Buddha's message travelled not just here, it went East too, crossed the seas and went South and South East to China. The great caves of Dunhuang which were so recklessly emptied by Aurel Stein; across then the forbidding wastes of the Takla-Makan, ('from which those that enter do not emerge'), across also the vast spread of the Gobi to Ulan Bator, then still travelling, ever moving,—North and East to Japan, to the shores of Lake Baikal, to the remote vastnesses of the autonomous Republic of Buryat, in today's Russia. There was no conquest here, only the spread of a thought, a faith, a belief, a pacifist conviction. No other thought has ever been able to spread so wide, so peacefully. But it is this 'pacifism' that ultimately also caused its demise. Violence uprooted and swept aside pacifism. Tragically, now only its ruins remain—of Buddhist buildings and statues and icons, all hauntingly beautiful and evocative—but most still only ruins, sad symbols, echoing their agony of destruction in this media driven world.

---

12. *Central Asia and India: The Formation and Development of Early Historical and Cultural Relations* by A.S. Sagdullaev, p. 14.
13. ibid.
14. ibid.

India was here as the Kushan legacy too. It was this legacy that influenced arts and became one of the 'foundations of the early medieval Sogdian civilization. A world of artistic subjects and images..........showing religious tolerance without dogmatic confessionalism',[15] and 'these Indian traditions were definitely integrated through the Kushans'. Some examples of these traditions are 'statuary images: Shiva and Nandi. The four armed goddess, whose avatar is depicted sitting on a dragon-like monster, providing evidence of the fact that the Indian traditions were organically integrated into the world of art and ideology of the Sogdian society'.[16]

Of course, in the wake of these gigantic sweeps of human thought great creativity also followed and flourished, till an 'alternative' arrived to displace the existing. That alternative was Islam. As a late arrival it has remained, but its creative impulse has now been sadly drained, there has crept in far too much slackness of thought, too much introversion; the assault of the Marxist doctrine too unrelenting, the influence of the West all pervasive and dominant. Oil revenues have finally drowned the great astronomers of Arabia. Not just Islam, the entire Orient has capitulated against the cultural, material, technological and military superiority of the Occident. But in Central Asia what silenced the genius of these people and their lands was the oppressive might of Moscow. Those great buildings—the mosques and madrasas and the soaring minarets, the arches, the sheer genius of Islamic architecture and colour (do you find 'phiroza', that unique blue anywhere else?) and craft got buried under mounds of Marxist, doctrinaire concrete.

What then of the conquerors? Some we have spoken of—the Huns, Scythians, and Mongols. The history of these lands, this entire region, resonates with the names that live in our consciousness, in India's particularly, even today—Alexander (or Sikander in India)

---

15. *Central Asia and India: Five Millenniums of Cultural Relations and Characteristics of Creative Interaction*, by V.M. Masson, p.10.
16. ibid.

and Changez and Taimur, and then of course, Babur, 'the only one who came and stayed', thus changing the course of Indian history.

It was to all this that I wanted to travel, to this 'crucible of mankind', with which India is so inseparably bound, still is; to these lands that had brought into Hindustan all these thoughts, forces, influences and conquerors, too. And to which lands in turn we had also given so much. What is it that lay beyond the Oxus—beyond our Amu Darya? What lands lay in the region of Transoxiana?

Also, from these lands had emerged Babur—who was this Babur? What forces caused him? From which land did he come; what impulse moved him, drove him irresistibly to 'Hindustan'? What of Uzbekistan? Where then was (is?) this 'Mughlistan'? For Babur had written he was not a 'Mughal'. That again had to be further searched, for the very foundations of our medieval history were being torn out, 'Babur not a Mughal'?

There was yet another factor. Why had no Indian traveller, other than that admirable and enterprising Mohan Lal Zutshi[17] (known much more commonly as just Mohan Lal or Mohan Lal Kashmiri) ever travelled to these lands? This, after all is where the silk road lay, horse traders constantly moved between Hindustan and here; other traders too went and returned but why none else just to travel, to see, to search? After all those 'admirable travelers of the 1820s and '30s, Moorcraft and Trebeck, Conolly, Pottinger, Richmond Shakespeare, Fraser—all these resourceful men', did travel so often and at such great risk 'amongst the tyrants and autocrats of pre-Russianised Turkestan'. Why then, not any of us Indians?

As a schoolboy, I had read of the defeat out of the British Expeditionary Force in Kabul, the catastrophe that had then met their retreat. I pored over narratives of the suffering of Stoddart and Conolly, their moving and horrifying ordeal. Why did they go there in the first instance? I so often wondered as a school boy.

---

17. Shri Mohan Lal, Esq. accompanied Sir Alexander Burnes on his journey to Bukhara in 1831-33. He liked to term himself thus, all this esq. and things.

'A few days later with their hands-bound, (they were) led into the great square before the Ark, or citadel, where stood the Emir's palace. What followed next, the Persian swore, he had learned from the executioner's own lips':[18]

'First, the two British officers were made to dig their own graves. Then they were ordered to kneel and prepare for death. Colonel Stoddart, was the first to be beheaded. Next the executioner turned to Conolly and informed him that the Emir had offered to spare his life if he would renounce Christianity and embrace Islam. Aware that Stoddart's forcible conversion had not saved him, Conolly, a devout Christian, declined. He then stretched out his neck for the executioner, and a moment later his head rolled in the dust beside that of his friend'.[19]

Map indicating the areas the author visited

18. *The Middle Years* by Henry James, p. 278.
19. *ibid*.

Twenty years later a poignant footnote was added to this. 'Through the post one day a small parcel arrived at the home of Conolly's sister in London. It contained the battered prayer book, which had been in her brother's possession throughout his captivity, and had evidently brought comfort to him and Stoddart during their long and painful ordeal. On the end papers and in the margins were penned in tiny hand details of their misfortunes. The last of these entries ended abruptly in mid-sentence. The prayer book had eventually found its way into the hands of a Russian living in St Petersburg who had managed to track down Conolly's sister'.[20] Sad to relate, this relic too, was subsequently lost.

It is for these and several other reasons all of which I could not myself identify, perhaps did not even know, but certainly in response to some deep rooted yearning that I finally set out on this journey— not as I would have wanted to—on foot or on horse back, in slow deliberate stages—one step at a time, savouring the land, the people, the change at every step. I had to go by aeroplane. It was the twentieth century.

---

20. ibid.

A Note on Babur

Zahiruddin Muhammad Babur (AD 1483–1530)

What unquenched thirst pushed Babur to search for his 'oasis' in Hindustan? What unattained goal, what quest brought him here to leave progeny that 'ruled', off and on, till the middle of the nineteenth century. The essentials are of course known; yet, what was his essence, his core? In this dim distance of centuries the answer is best found in Babur's own writing in the *Baburnama*, a truly remarkable chronicle.

Zahiruddin Muhammad Babur, (AD 1483-1530), born in Fergana in Transoxiana (modern Uzbekistan and Tajikistan), a scion of the dynasty that had reigned undisputed throughout eastern Iran and Central Asia since the time of Amir Temür

Emperor Babur

(AD 1336-1405), enthroned on Samarkand at the age of twelve, emerged as a 'Timurid ruler when there were too many claimants to too few thrones'. Driven from his homeland 'he spent a lifetime winning kingdoms and losing a few along the way', gradually moving south from modern Uzbekistan and Tajikistan, through Afghanistan, to the Indian subcontinent, thus successively becoming the ruler in Kabul and in parts of Hindustan. He certainly did 'expand the boundaries of the Timuried cultural sphere' and 'founded in 1526, what eventually became the Mughal Empire'.

It has often been suggested that 'Babur means tiger; it has, in fact, nothing to do with the Persian word Babur, tiger'. Mirza Muhammad Haydar explains how Babur was given his nickname: 'At that time the Chaghatai were very rude and uncultured, and not refined as they are now; thus they found [his given name] Zahir-ud-Din Muhammad difficult to pronounce, and for this reason gave him the name of [Babur]'.[21]

'He was adorned with various virtues, and clad with numberless good qualities, above all of which bravery and humanity had the ascendant'.[22] Known to history primarily as the progenitor of the 'Grand Mughals' of India, Babur was, ironically, a man of whom it has been said that[23] 'nothing in his life was Indian, except possibly, the leaving of it'. In fact, Babur found everything about the subcontinent other than its riches, distasteful. He was accustomed to the society of Transoxiana and the beautiful landscape and climate of Kabul and longed to return to his beloved Kabul, a trip he made only posthumously.[24]

---

21. Muhammad Haydar Dughlat. *A History of the Moghuls of Central Asia*, p.9. Trans.E. Denison Ross, ed.and annot. Ney Elias (London: Sampson Law, Marstan, 1898: reissue, New York: Praeger Publications, 1970), p.9.
22. ibid.
23. Muhammad Haydar Dughlat. *A History of the Moghuls of Central Asia*, p. 173 & Forster. *Emperor Babur*, p. 304.
24. ibid.

There is then his connection with Changez and Taimur. For us, though, unfortunately Genghis Khan's centuries-old negative image remains. However, in 'fifteenth-century Central Asia, Genghisid descent was a powerful legitimizing factor. Where Genghisids reigned, their right to rule was unquestioned. Even where rulers were not descended from Genghis, as in Timuried, Genghisid protocol was observed. This was acknowledged by Babur, too'.[25]

There is another complexity. Babur rejects being called a Mughal.[26] 'Although the word Moghul, employed in the *Baburnama* and elsewhere for the Turkicized descendants of Genghis Khan's Mongols, is originally the same as Mongol, Moghulistan also means Mongolia proper'; this is retained as "Moghul" and "Moghulistan" to distinguish the Chaghatayid Turks of Moghulistan from the Mongols of today's Mongolia, who do not figure at all in Babur's writings'. For us, in India, this is almost heretical, which is why such assertions intrigued me greatly. How do I find the correct answer?

Around the beginning of the 'fourteenth century, the Chaghatayids nominally converted to Islam, although, since they surrounded themselves with the trappings of their quasi-Buddhist, quasi-shamanistic past, the wilder elements in the east continued to appear half-pagan to the fervent Muslim populations of Samarkand and Bukhara, who called them Moghuls'.[27] Babur reflects 'the same attitude of the civilised urbanite towards the uncivilised steppe peoples in his descriptions of Moghuls'—even of his uncle: 'Sultan-Ahmad Khan, the Khan of eastern Moghulistan', whose tent he wrote: 'looked like a robber's den—melons and grapes and horse trappings strewn all over'[28] and says of the Moghuls: 'most of [them]

---

25. Genghisid and Timurid Background of *Baburnama*; p. 25, pub. Oxford University Press, NY.
26. Rene Grousset. *The Empire of the Steppes* (New Brunswick:Rutgers University Press, 1970 pp. 326-28.
27. ibid.
28. ibid.

had never possessed or even lived in a village—nay, had never even seen cultivation. They were as wild as the beasts of the mountains'.[29] In Babur's time the Moghuls spoke Turkish—it is extremely unlikely that many of them knew Mongolian at all—'and the descendants of the original Mongol tribes and garrisons that had come into the area were indistinguishable from their neighbouring Turkic tribesmen'.[30]

We are also informed that 'Moghulistan had become a recognizable entity shortly after 1340 CE, when the Chaghatayid Khanate split into two branches, one in Transoxiana under Qazan Khan (c 1343-46), whose descendants fell into a position subordinate to Turkic tribal lords of the sort typified by Amir Temür, and the other in 'Moghulistan.' There was a blood relationship with Taimur, on his father's side. 'Babur's great-great-grand father, Amir Temür, made .... conquests ranging from India to Anatolia'. Yet, despite his 'extraordinary power during his own (Temür's) lifetime Genghisid legitimacy was unquestioned', and he (Temürs) was 'careful to rule through a puppet Genghisid Khan, as many of his predecessors in the Ulus Chaghatay had done before him'. After Temür's death, however, the 'Timurids ruled in their own right in Khurasan and Transoxiana, without the benefit of Genghisid legitimisation'.[31] In fact, by the end of the fifteenth century, in a 'curious replay of history, the Timurids had taken the role of the Genghisids and Turkic warlords used Timurid princes like Babur to legitimise their *de facto* rule of provinces'.[32] Just how far the relationship between the Timurids and Genghisids had been reversed from what it once was is well illustrated by the words Sultan-Abusa id Mirza addressed to Yunus Khan before he sent him into Moghulistan.

'Since I have ascended the throne, my power is so absolute that I have no need of a Khan; so now I have divested you of the garments

---

29. *History of the Mughuls* by Muhammad Haydar Dughlat. p. 153.
30. *Baburnama* by Babur.
31. ibid. Translator's Preface, p. 20.
32. ibid.

of poverty and, having clothed you in princely robes, am sending you back to your native country on the following conditions: For the future you must not follow the example of your ancestors and say— 'Amir Timur and the race of Amir Timur are our vassals, and have been for generations.' For although it was formerly so, things have changed now, and I am *padishah* in my own right; thus, now if you are going to be my vassal, you must bear the name of "servitor" and do away with the name of "friend". There is a direct communication for you'.

Historians often comment that Babur was robbed 'of his fame as a Central Asian and sovereign over the kingdom of Kabul', where he 'ruled for much longer than in India', but also of his 'primary identity as a Timurid' by labelling him and his successors as 'Mughals'—that is, 'Moghuls, or Mongols—an appellation that would not have pleased him in the least. In India the dynasty always called itself Gurkani, after Temir's title Gurkan, the Persianised form of the Mongolian *kuragan*, son-in-law, a title he assumed after his marriage to a Genghisid princess'. Nonetheless, Europeans, recognising that there was some connection between Babur's house and the Mongols, but ignorant of the precise relationship, dubbed the dynasty with some variant of the misnomer Moghul (Mongol, Mogul, Monghol, etc.) and made that name 'synonymous with greatness'. (Translator's Preface from *Baburnama*).

On his attaining kingship Babur records in the *Baburnama*. 'Thus, in the month of Ramadan in the year 899 (June 1494), in the province of Fergana, in my twelfth year I became king'.

What reveals the personality of Babur far more clearly is his letter to Humayun, quoted only in part here. It is a classic, a ruler's advice to his successor, a father's to his son, a King's to his heir and prince.

Babur's letter to his son Humayun

'Thinking of you with much longing, I greet you. My words are these: on Monday the tenth of Rabi (Novembr 23),

Begina and Buyan Shaykh came. From your letters and reports we have become acquainted with the situation on both sides of the Hindu Kush.

I give thanks for your son, a son to you and a beloved one to me.

May God ever grant me and you such joy. Amen, O Lord of the Universe. You have named him "al-Aman." May God bless him. However, although you yourself may write it thus, you have not considered the fact that frequently the common people will say either "Alaman" or "Ilaman." Moreover, names with "al-" are rare. Nonetheless, may God bless and keep both him and his name, for my sake and yours, may He keep al-Aman in fortune and happiness for many years, for many decades. God has ordered our affairs through his great grace and generosity. Such an event has not happened in how many decades?

Item: On Tuesday the eleventh, rumours were heard to the effect that the people of Balkh had summoned Qurban and let him in.

Item: Kamran and the Kabul Beg were ordered to go join you, and you all will proceed to Hissar or Samarkand or whichever direction is in our best interests. Through God's grace you will defeat your enemies, take their territory, and make your friends happy by overthrowing the foe. God willing, this is your time to risk your life and wield your sword. Do not fail to make the most of an opportunity that presents itself.

Indolence and luxury do not suit kingship. Conquest tolerates not inaction: the world is his who hastens most. When one is master one may rest from everything—except being king.

In your letters you keep talking about being alone. Solitude is a flaw in kingship, as has been said, 'If you are fettered, resign yourself; but if you are a lone rider, your reins are free.'

There is no bondage like the bondage of kingship. In kingship it is improper to seek solitude.

As I asked, you have written your letters, but you didn't read them over, for if you had had a mind to read them, you would have found that you could not. After reading them you certainly would have changed them. Although your writing can be read with difficulty, it is excessively obscure. Who has ever heard of prose designed to be an enigma? Your spelling is not bad, although it is not entirely correct either.

Your handwriting can be made out somehow or other, but with all these obscure words of yours the meaning is not entirely clear. Probably your laziness in writing letters is due to the fact that you try to make it too fancy. From now on write with uncomplicated, clear, and plain words. This will cause less difficulty both for you and for your reader'.

A Post-Script

By driving out the Islamised Tartars of the 'Golden Horde' Russia asserted its Imperial domain into the very heart of the Central Asian Khanates. When therefore, Moscow was swallowed by a Marxist revolution, inevitably its 'Central Asian Empire' too had to follow suite. Rapidly, the Emirs and others of the Khanates got eliminated; Islam then came under siege. The uncaring heel of change crushed all dissent, the muezzein fell silent, countless numbers of mosques were razed or sealed or put to some other 'secular' use, or were simply abandoned. 'Azaan', that had called the faithful to prayer for so many centuries now no longer echoed across the sands here. Muslims became Marxists; and the 'ism' of Marx became the new faith. Tyranny of the 'Khans' continued, only their identity was now different, though, they too, sat (mostly) in Moscow. Time passed, and yet again the wheel turned; as the twentieth century began to wind down, occurred another great transformation. This was the collapse and disintegration of the USSR. The doctrine of Marx, which had emerged so forcefully on the ruins of a Czarist Russia, which had at one time won so many million adherents, lost its convictions and that too with startling suddenness. Yesterday's devotees and communist idolaters overnight became unforgiving 'idol breakers'. Not ever in the history of human thought had a concept like maxism so dominated so many, and then, within the span of just one lifetime collapsed so suddenly, so totally.

These ancient lands of Central Asia were 'free' again. The suddenness of it all, of this transformation, caused many traumas—of national identity, of governance, about faith. Islam reemerged, not perhaps whole but certainly far more aggressively assertive then before.

My journey was to see and experience Islamic lands under Marxist totalitarianism, that also was my purpose. All that is now part of history. The relevance of the journey, of the questions with which I went—and their answers—whether found or not, remains.

Tashkent

(Uzbek or Marxist?)

The flight was late in leaving. I was in error to have assumed that a machine like perfection obtained, simply because it was a USSR owned Aeroflot, therefore, everything would happen efficiently, with an efficiency not ordinarily to be expected from the imperfect world of democracy. But this was utterly naïve. A 9 a.m. departure eventually took place around at 11.00 a.m.—of course, there were no announcements on the causes of delay, nor any expressions of even feigned regret, no explanations either, just an overwhelming, totalitarian silence. Patiently all of us sat in the lounge, most being Soviet citizens, resigned and uncomplaining. I, fuming and angry, but wisely only inwardly. The Illushyin was half full. The rest of the seats, with what I could only term as 'communist practicality', were loaded with cargo. An anxious frontier flying atmosphere prevailed inside the aircraft, reminiscent to me of the early cargo flying years of Jam-Air in upper Assam. No seat reservations—sit where you like, rather where you can find one. I am sandwiched between a Russian woman of the usual proportions and a timid fellow countryman with halitosis. The air hostesses are uniformly unwelcoming. An absence of refinement inside the aircraft.

We take off smoothly, and through scudding clouds bank, turn, climb again, then head north. Though it is but just midday, the tension of the preceding days and the workload that I have had to carry is drained out of me. I nod off.

Suddenly I am shaken by the arm and rudely woken up. It is the air hostess performing her gentle functions. 'Refreshments?' she enquires. I look at the watch, for over an hour I have been between sleep and wakefulness. I think of what they would all be doing back home at that hour—just coming on to midday. A sandwich, an optional apple, exactly four biscuits and tea or coffee, difficult to distinguish which is which, arrive.

Mountains of astounding cragginess, just below the starboard wing over which I sit. A landscape almost lunar in its bleak inhospitality and just around the top of this range of mountains, occasionally a line, just a smudge of white, late and obstinate remains of summer snow. Otherwise all of it is an unrelieved, uniform sandy brown, the rocks, too, are of the same shade, perhaps a touch darker. Shadows cast by fleeting clouds leave stark pools of contrast, momentarily creating an illusion of vegetation. The mountains slowly recede and we are again over an unbelievably uniform wasteland of a desert. Over what are we currently flying? I wonder but am too timid to enquire from these daunting amazons, miscalled hostesses.

Before our descent to Tashkent begins, as Glazebrook, has observed in his *Journey to Khiva:* 'a glimpse of the rock and snow of the Tien Shan again in a curious fierce light, then cloud again dropped over the by now distant scene, and there was only the bluish haze hanging above Tashkent's trees, and deeper mist beyond'.

Life and greenery then make a first, tentative appearance in the valleys that lie groined between brown mountains, like an occasional sprinkling of parsley. Nearer Tashkent, agriculture finally appears, large collectivised fields, with hut like dots filling space, of what I can only assume are villages.

All, certainly almost all airports in the world, have the detritus of urban living spread around them, expanding contagiously like fungus. The slums of Santa Cruz, the shabby suburbs around Heathrow, and the forgotten villages around Palam, they are all of the same genre; Tashkent is not any exception. We land almost literally through the backyard of communism's private enterprise. Small holdings, defiant backyards really, sprouting corn and an occasional vegetable patch, valiantly resisting this levelling out process of collectivisation. Ominously, and to my jaundiced eye with typical communist insensitivity, there lies an aeroplane junkyard just adjacent to the taxing runway. Another might well call it 'practical', which perhaps it is, if you happen to reason that the best place to dump the junk of crashed aircraft is in the available space next to an airfield. But it certainly is not best for the morale of flying passengers. Along the airport's rim also lies a haphazard jumble of concrete slabs—Is it for safety? I wonder.

We enter an empty arrival hall, where all are asked to wait. No one knows why or is able to explain even to the few who ask. The airport staff merely volunteer: 'wait a few minutes'. So we all stand, impatiently or resignedly, but all certainly uncomfortable and all clutching our awkward aircraft loads. The Tashkent passengers are then asked to proceed through empty, echoing halls. Action at last, I think with relief. At the immigration and passport control there is just one woman, in the smock of a health official. She asks for my passport, looks at it, makes some notes and gives it back.

After what I thought was a polite wait I ask: 'Well, what are we waiting for?' 'Wait'—I am informed, rather commanded, curtly but conclusively. She yells at somebody behind a closed door and slowly some people troop out from various nooks and corners of the airport; 'Not unlike cockroaches', I think in my uncharitable frame of mind. Then in one of those truly astounding but typically bureaucratic decisions, we are informed that those of us who are disembarking at Tashkent are to wait further until those transiting to Moscow have not gone through. Why then were we asked to precede them in the first instance? I enquire this of no one in particular, rather irreverently and judging from the response that I get, clearly also irrelevantly because there is no response still. Some more impatient waiting follows. This screening of the transit passengers takes forever, or so it seems to those of us who are waiting. We are all 'fairly in the clutches now, what does Moscow have to fear', I wonder. There are only about ten of us disembarking at Tashkent. Of them five are Indians: an elderly, bespectacled Bengali, a primary school teacher, I think to myself; a Bengali lady in a beautiful natural colour silk sari, two rather indeterminate Maharashtrians, one of whom is already inquiring of the other, details that the timid always ask of their fellow travellers. Then, self—already beginning to feel somewhat pompous. They tell me they they are a part of this unending 'Indo-Soviet friendship delegation' routine. Do not appear very friendly to the USSR, though.

At last it is our turn. Deliberately I hum a rather insolent and irreverent tune as the officials scrutinise my passport. Then to Customs. We have to fill yet another form. All around are billboards giving details of regulations, and all variety of fearful warnings. The form—which in structure and content appears very familiar—what with its emphasis on the number of bags (including hand bags) and currency declarations and such other, not always heeded injunctory details. The theory being: treat everyone as a suspect, a potential criminal; in any event tie up everyone (metaphorically only, though) through such a diverse variety of written documents that the state can trip them, rather trip any one, now or later, or whenever it so chooses. Therefore, laboriously and with great diligence, I set to filling out the form. An official rushes up: 'Mr. Singh, you are holding a diplomatic passport?'—'Yes'—'No, no, no need to fill up form. It does not apply to you.' Laws do not apply to 'us'. The state is 'us'; everyone else is 'them'. I do not believe I am also 'us'. I know now that of course, this is where customs and immigration officials, back home, have learnt their trade, down to the format and the contents of the 'form' itself.

A pleasant faced Intourist man accosts me. 'There is no car yet but one has been sent for from the Hotel. You are staying at Hotel

Uzbekistan'. I am relieved to learn that I am expected. He looks at my Intourist Voucher which represents my single, rather tenuous link of access to lodgings; an improbable umbilical cord of legitimacy this. 'You are holding a diplomatic passport; are you in the government?'

'No, I am not, I oppose it,' I say with practised flippancy. This is met by silence, total non response, somewhat embarrassed, though not entirely unsympathetic.

'What is your name?' I enquire to conciliate this pleasant young man on whom I have needlessly practised my cleverness.

'Fazur Rehman' I repeat the name in genuine, pleased surprise. He looks up at me shyly, smiles knowingly, as if he both knows of and understands the kinship that I am attempting to establish by my pleased surprise; and then he actually winks at me. I kept wondering for long afterwards—why?

'Do you work for Intourist?' an unnecessary question but I am trying to go beyond the confines of the system; to its human content.

'Yes. I work one day and have three off.'

'My God', (that reference to the Almighty in this land of state enforced atheism was purely reflex not any deliberate provocation), 'you mean you actually get three days off for one day's work?'

My question, I realise the moment I have asked it, is again tactless and is bound to embarrass young Fazur Rehman.

'Why? Would you not want to do such work?' he defends weakly.

'No,' I am emphatic. 'You could hardly be making enough for a living.'

FR is silent. Is it my deliberate, rather insensitive probing or have I touched a raw nerve of discontent and truth somewhere?

'We young have to be grateful for even this work', is finally his resigned reply, after a prolonged silence. But by then our conversation has got too close to the bone. FR gently draws me to another portion of the hall where we cannot be overheard. Or, is this 'one day out of three', a subterfuge for statistics and for keeping unemployment down?

While we are waiting for the car to arrive, FR scrutinises my itinerary and wonders why Intourist has given me such a complex way of doing that which is rather straightforward. I then ask him why I have been given a boarding card?—for that is what the Passport control has given me. It transpires that 'the system' has fumbled again. Though my visa does not say so, the officials at the desk have routinely given me one letter because the Moscow lot preceded me and the officials thought that that is where I belonged too, or because they just assumed that a 'diplomat' passport must go to Moscow! Either way this great security apparatus fumbled—again.

The car in which I travel, is of some strange make but is almost entirely American in design. And these asphalt roads do not belong to Central Asia, they are wide and relatively free of traffic. There is the usual jumping of lights, I observe. Possibly because it is Saturday and there just could not be any rush hour in Tashkent.

Temperature is in the thirties and warm. People, dark haired, olive complexioned, sandaled and so very North Indian in demeanour and looks. Blood red channels on traffic islands. Walnut, Chinar[33] and Poplar, strikingly like Kashmir—so this is what Babur had transported, it was nostalgia for this land that made him yearn for home. The great 'Chinar' too, is from Uzbekistan—so at least they say. Is it? I wonder.

At the hotel more bureaucracy and more form filling. A faceless, tasteless public building, all concrete and stone and just as unfeeling. The room, a poky little alcove with dirty toilets; though there is a paper ring informing, without much conviction, that all this has all been 'sanitised'. Everything takes so long, like getting one's baggage, or changing money, where arbitrary rates are the order, or even getting food. Hotel shops are full of touristy 'rubbish', touted as 'local handicraft', 'folk dances' at teatime, are advertised as the 'best of the Republic'.

There is also an immensely sad looking orchestra playing something even more depressing with the bandsman in an unimaginative

---

33. 'Chinar'—Botanically known as *Platanus Orientails*.

'workmen's blue'. Tables adjacent to mine are laden with fruit and Russian Champagne and Vodka and mineral water and Coca Cola. Nan is 'Non', and there is 'Pulao', with mutton and 'Shorba'–a soup and 'Chaval'–threads of continuity from a deeper and in some sense, a more essential past tug at me.

By my table are some really rough looking Vodka swillers. Perhaps they are a drilling rig crew who have earned special holiday vouchers, (so much seems to happen here on the strength of this ubiquitous voucher), I think to myself. But they are undoubtedly some variety of favoured citizens. That is why one of them so incongruously and almost sacrilegiously is wearing a shirt marked 'U.S. Army'—and another proudly sports an 'Adidas' cotton knit, a girl attempts, or rather apes military chic by wearing 'US Marines'. The girls are alas, ...the Islamic influence is too patent, also somewhat reminiscent of Iran but with a certain additional heaviness. There are touches of America, too, in the henna coloured hair and then something from the more northern, colder regions of Mongolia. This mixture is more sad than attractive; a certain lack of style is obvious enough, for the dress styles and the manner of wearing them, both in men and women, are forced, also borrowed for they are an adaptation, not at all native or natural, not harmonious; in consequence, everyone so attired attains, in my eyes, an unhappy and undignified manner. The total effect on women is not soft as it ordinarily is and ought to be with feminity, and on men it is characterlessness as it ought not to be. Near by, on another table sits a hulk of a Mongol, a wrestler, I think. And I muse on the effects of this all pervading 'ism' on native societies.

It is only great sweeps of religions that help form societies. Take any example: the giant Islamic sweep of the southern fringes of the Soviet Republic, (which in reality is an Empire) in all of them whether Turkmen, Uzbek, Tajik, or Kirghiz, it is Islam that has moulded societies. Further afield, the influence of Buddha's thought unfurls like a giant umbrella over Mongolia, Tibet, China or Japan creating a lifestyle. Equally so, the near inerasable engraving of orthodox Christianity on a 'European' Russia, and others—say the Baltics—it is this that has moulded social norms. In all these lands, societies themselves evolved an order, a lifestyle and cultivated their cultural norms all in the wake of religious thought, and also as a consequence of it. Only religion has that resource of thought and reflection which can sustain societies. It is the only thought force that is able to withstand the ravages of time and pestilence and war and destitution, too. The communist creed has certainly created a state administration, also fiscal and political systems. But it cannot, does not, nurture in its arid heart the seeds of the growth and flowering of a civilisation. That is its central absence. In ethical and philosophical terms communism conceptualises everything, but only on the material plane. Should its state apparatus, thereafter, ever fail to deliver the material sustenance (e.g. now in Poland)*, it will flounder. More tellingly significant to me in a historical sense is that communism can never be a civilisational concept, will not be.

Why otherwise, in this land of 'dialectical materialism', has the assault of the 'culture of the blue jean and rock band' so clearly triumphed? Witness, too, the patent inequalities that remain, say between the woman who swabbed the hotel floor, did the room, served at the table and the 'US Marine', or the curious and sad 'gentility' of a more than middle-aged assistant at the Intourist desk; the difference in 'attitudes' between the waiters, the porter, the taxi driver and the smugness and the self-satisfied air of those who obviously belong to the 'apparatus', those that have managed to become 'us', as separate from 'them'. This is the same, as in any other system, the world over.

After dinner, I ventured out of the hotel for a stroll around the park that lay in front. A granite statue on an obelisk. Trees crowded with chattering birds. 'In Tashkent's trees fluttered... swifts and magpies; their presence here fixing the geography, an extension southward of the northern hemisphere', describes Glazebrook.

---

*Note: This account is of a period in the early 1980s.

Tashkent has through the centuries been, and still is, a great meeting point of continents—Europe and Asia, the Northern Continental regions and the Southern peninsular lands; trade routes from the East and from the West, all converge here. The old silk and gold routes passed through Tashkent. Czarist Russia moved the seat of its Uzbek Empire from Samarkand to this city. For the USSR, it became the capital of the Uz SSR (Uzbek Soviet Socialist Republic). Architecturally, it is a confused kind of a sprawl, somewhat of a mix between 'Mediterranean Europeanism' and the 'Central Asian Islam', three separate and discernible layers of influence exist side by side, almost three distinctly separate cities. There is that old Central Asian confusion of a city, mud huts and an untidy sprawl of hovels and tight, narrow alleys. Uzbeks squat comfortably besides their donkey carts while mongrels scratch in rubbish heaps. Also those empty mosques, of contrasting clay, and that incomparable Islamic 'phiroza' (blue), and domes and soaring minarets from atop which the muezzein once upon a time summoned the faithful. The mosques are there, so too are the minarets but no 'azaan' is heard here now. Then came this Czarist Europeanisation. Just where old Tashkent ends a new city came into being. Like any imperial power, the conquerors built themselves a city of their own design, for their comfort only. Here there is, (like Lutyens' New Delhi or the civil lines in any of the Indian towns, also the cantonments), a deliberate withdrawal (separation) from the lifestyle of the ruled. Elegant villas, reminiscent of some long forgotten European South, with tree lined boulevards, gardens, and straight, spacious avenues, where, I imagine, officers of the Czar perhaps took their evening air in elegant carriages whilst the subject Uzbeks duly and respectfully salaamed (or were made to.) There is not any such 'entire Czarist quarter' now left intact. The great earthquake (1966) took away so much, only some examples remain, 'pleasant cool buildings on a neo-classical plan, a portico of white Ionic columns flanked by wings colour-washed in yellow ochre, its dentil frieze, and its window cases, and broken pediment, each adding the interest of patterned shade to the façade'.[34] It is only in these remnants of buildings that faint echoes of a Czarist past can still faintly be heard.

And then came the age of 'Communist grandeur'. Outdoing their Czarist predecessors, from the ruins of the catastrophic earthquake of 1966, was created a city of grand monuments, to awe and to inspire. The might of the Soviet Republic poured into creating a city of such splendour as had never earlier been seen in Central Asia. Fountains play symbolically in the shape of a cotton flower, or in memory of that tradition which informs that this was once an oasis, as a cascade in the shape of waterfall. There are theatres of magnificent opulence with marbles of many hues brought from Samarkand. Shade trees line the easy on traffic roads and squares are filled with shrubbery and flowers. In this Republic, no one is to be left unemployed, not statistically, in any event; so labour for attending to such chores is plentiful. Shops of some unexpected finery and renowned fruits abound. There are queues, however, outside a shop selling cotton textiles and in the bazaar there stands the by now familiar sight of an impatient line of buyers for meat.

For the fourth largest city of the Republic (1.5 million) the public transportation system works, trams and buses and 'We have a metro'— Abdul Momeen had informed me with justifiable pride.

'Why do people buy cars then?' It is a mean question. I get a dialectical reply: 'It is a manifestation of bourgeois mentality.' I wait as if expecting him to complete what he has started; something like 'the socialist revolution is yet not complete', etc. He too pauses, and then adds, to my delighted astonishment:

'Because in a car we can go where we like and when we like but a bus may go only there and there and there.'

But then Tashkent is also the Communist city of lifeless concrete blocks put together as buildings, shapeless, tasteless and utterly lacking in the smallest spark of humanity. From the pulsating squalor and confusion of the old slums of Tashkent, remnants of which still

---

34. *Journey to Khiva* by Phillip Glazebrook, p.72; pub. Kodansha International

exist, people were herded out and forced in to these faceless concrete monstrosities. It is always difficult to decide which is worse—the squalor of state servitude or that which is the consequence of the individual's license.

'How many people died in the great quake of 1966?' I asked.
'Fifteen were killed and 365 injured,' pat came the reply.
'Only fifteen? In such a major quake?'
'Yes, you see, 'AM patiently but futilely attempts the official lie, 'it was the month of April, quite warm, and in Central Asia people have the habit of sleeping out.'

Why do totalitarian states always attempt to cloak the full extent of natural or man-made disasters? Because nature, in its fury, brings to light the impotence of the state, exposing all claims of omnipotence.

After a pause, AM then politely enquires:
'Mr. Singh do you mind if I ask you some questions?'
'No, no, do Abdul, feel free to ask anything.'
'Is the Communist party very popular in India?'
'No.'
'You are in Parliament. Is your leader Rajeshwar Rao?'[35]
'No.'
'What do you do in the Parliament then, Mr. Singh?'
'I oppose the government.' I knew we were entering areas of some relative incomprehension here, that I would face problems.
'You mean you are alone? An individual?'

There are so many answers to both these truthful, genuine queries. I am at a loss about where to start. I take the soft option—but I am also (shamefully) somewhat patronising: 'Look Abdul, you will not understand. In India we need not all agree with the government—we can follow the line that we believe in. We have many political parties.'

---

35. Rajeshwar Rao was a Rajya Sabha member from Andhra Pradesh belonging to the Communist Party of India.

'Yes, we too had the Socialist revolutionaries, and they made a mess of things, and the people threw them out, and we now have the Communist party whom the people want.' AM, in the attitude of QED.

Inevitably, I think of home and the pronouncements back home but remain silent.

'The Communist party has sixteen million members. In Uzbekistan we have six hundred thousand. I am a member,' announces AM with a rightly felt pride 'The Communist party lays down the policy, which the people follow.'

'What is the population of USSR?' 'It is a trap', I feel like shouting, cautioning AM, but it is already too late, answers learnt by rote arrive instantly.

'The rate of growth of population in Uzbekistan is three times that in Russia. In all we are 268 million people.'

'And how many did you say are members of the party?'

'Sixteen million.'

'And they tell the rest what to do?' We are now standing in front of the Uzbekistan Parliament.

'No,' followed by a long explanation of the theory of the Soviet Constitution, etc., then that grand simplification as a finale:

'In this building (pointing to the Parliament) decisions are taken and then they are sent to that building—(where the all powerful, faceless bureaucracy sits, I assume) from where they are implemented.'

It is an imposing square, free of traffic, people with the unmistakable stamp of 'being something' stroll about. By the side of Lenin's statue is the old Parliament—a pleasing colonial structure. In a corner of it a granite plaque, to mark that it is in this building that FM Ayub Khan and Lal Bahadur Shastri conferred, in 1966.[36]

---

36. The prime minister of India, Shri Lal Bhadur Shastri and the president of Pakistan, Field Marshall Ayub Khan on 10 January 1966 signed an agreement at Tashkent to restore normal and peaceful relations and to promote understanding and friendly relations between their peoples. This was to resolve issues consequent to the armed conflict in September 1965. Tragically Shri Lal Bhadur Shastri died of a heart attack the next day while still at Tashkent.

Seeing it I am yet again struck by the symbolism of Russia choosing Tashkent as the venue of their 'mediatory' efforts between India and Pakistan. Was the effort 'mediatory', or was it a not so cloaked assertion of the natural right and power of this country— a manifestation of the imperial might of the USSR? Did we not, India and Pakistan, commit an appalling error in ever agreeing to the USSR playing this role, and above all, to it being played in the capital of Imperialist Russia's central Asian Empire? When one travels in Central Asia, and sitting as I do now in Tashkent, I am struck again by the strength of this impression. 'Did they not then think along such lines?' I wonder inwardly. In 1965-66, I was in uniform but had even then questioned what was being done. USSR is the twentieth century's mightiest imperial power, and the greatest failure of Tashkent lay in our inability to even comprehend the inherent symbolism.

'Tell me, Mr. Singh,' we are driving to Shastri's memorial, 'is there any barrier to inter-faith marriage, any colour prejudice in India?' AM asks. I do want to answer honestly.

'Yes. We have several religions, then there is a caste factor too, and colour is not un-important. And what about you?'

'With us the government says....'

'Forget the government. Abdul, tell me what you think.'

'Well, the policy of the Republic...'

'Not the policy, Abdul, the reality.'

He waits until the car has come to a halt and we have stepped out to walk towards Shastri's bust. 'Well, to tell you the truth, the Russian like to live with Russians and the Uzbek with Uzbek, Tajiks amongst their own, so also the Kirghiz etc. But since 1986 we now have many peoples from the other Republics here, living in Uzbekistan.' AM is an honest communist. Back at the hotel, when we return he gives me a whole sheaf of 'literature' to read. Amongst them is—*The Truth About Afghanistan*.

'Why Afghanistan?' I enquire.

'Well, so that you can come to know facts.'

I have come to like AM. An Asian courtesy and gentleness of manner, also befitting deference defines his behaviour. This morning at Bukhara, the porter who had come to collect my baggage, being imbued with centuries of feudal observances, had knocked on the door, respectfully, and when I opened the door bowed and waited. For him it is easy to accept one master in place of another—one Sultan in his fort (a commissioner in the inspiring administrative building), a Czar in distant Moscow—and he, a simple Uzbek or Tajik in his place. So this order of the world has continued, and all the while the patient, squatting denizens of Central Asia have always known, for the past many millennia now, that all this is a simple, an elementary, inerasable fact of life.

Lal Bahadur Shastri's small, simple bust is placed on a not very tall pedestal, surrounded by a newly planted grove of trees. It is dappled by sunlight and shadow as I walk up to it. This junction of roads on which the memorial is placed is fairly busy. It appears to be an important traffic point. The whole effect is simple and unimposing but not without charm. Despite the busy traffic around it, this grove manages to exude an atmosphere of tranquillity and some peace. Shastri's bust appears to be smiling. Just behind the grove are some nondescript buildings. A gravel path leads up to the bust and obliquely around it. I am struck by no particular emotion as I walk up to it. In any case I know that this is not the spot of his death. When I enquire from Abdul where that place is, he is vague. When I point out that it was in a dacha outside Tashkent, he says 'Yes, it is some official spot about twenty-five kilometers from here.'

I do not know for how long I can keep this up? It is again 1 a.m. in the morning. Later today I am to leave for Ferghana. That would be a relief. Tashkent too is full of tourists—Mongols (drunk), an oily and obsequious Afghan, officials being banqueted with laden tables, and tourists from 'friendly socialist countries'—all in the name of 'peace, friendship and solidarity'. Even some ancient Japanese and a group of Canadians and Americans in orthopaedic walking shoes.

They were travelling courtesy 'Harmony Travels', and had just returned from the solar eclipse at Bratsk.

'Are there any tourists in Kokand?' I ask of the Intourist man.

'Oh Kokand, no one goes to Kokand.'

'Why? It is such an ancient city?'

'No, no there is nothing in Kokand.'

It is to Kokand and to Ferghana and Bukhara and Khiva and that jewel of old, Samarkand therefore, that I look forward very much to going.

So transparent and so patently obvious is the true nature of the Soviet state, it is clearly a state 'communist totalitarian autocracy.' It is not progressive in its economic structure, it is expansionist and it is imperial, reflecting 'old historic aims, of (an) imperial Russia'. My 'outer cognition', has almost imperceptibly turned to an inner understanding and conviction.

My diary notes get longer and longer, both in the time that they take to formulate as describable ideas, and then even longer to distil them into 'connected' reference points. The latter is not always possible. The mind jumps at will, takes over, and then I am compelled to write or note whatever it dictates. Also when I sit to write, it takes a long, long time to find that starting point; the needed trigger to grasp that end of the thread which once picked up will enable me to easily and effortlessly keep on pulling in a manner that has both elegance and flow, until the whole then unravels as a masterly, deductive and convincingly logical thesis. Wonderful in theory, so far removed from reality, though. So often the mind turns totally blank and the eyes keep staring at an empty sheet of paper. Today, for instance, it is near midnight before I am able to even begin writing.

Travelogue writing is not, can simply not be like an instant snap-shot; it is not such an exercise. Though ordinarily an anxiety ridden traveller, here in the USSR, I am the most relaxed of that variety. Principally because I have transferred (in-reality, because of no option) the responsibility of seeing me on board the aircraft to the state, to Intourist. 'I have not one minute in life, not one minute

I tell you,' complained my old guide Usmanov Egitaly (UE) when yet again he arrived late. He had volunteered to do my 'seeing off', bumping someone higher in the ladder of reservations in the process. It was good to see him again; also reassuring to find him the same. He had time nevertheless to sit down and write me a card, which he later presented. 'When three groups come I go mad and all for 150 Rbls. I tell you! I say have one more guide. They say no. As if Russia will go poor if it had to employ one more guide. We spend millions on...' I can't hear on what. I am being rushed to the aircraft, where by the boarding ladders on the tarmac, Egitaly embraces me and kisses me on both cheeks. I could not have had a fonder farewell from Uzbekia.

I do not want to be a 'Malice in Wonderland'; I do not also want to be patronising or cynically sneer at the staggering material advancements that have been made by the Russian state system. But I incline to the view that the communist doctrine perhaps had less to do with this than the totalitarianism imposed on a war torn land and on a starving peasantry. If any negation of the 'Marxist doctrine' were needed, it was at the point of origin of the Great October Revolution itself. It occurred in a feudal, agricultural state not as a result of the rise and awakening of any 'proletariat' or the 'working classes'. No, it followed a pattern; a pattern of historical evolution, a 'cyclical theory' of historical developments. Almost like a chemical reaction, in a given time and circumstance, a certain course of events will occur, almost like a chemical chain of events; because it is inevitable, it is predictable. Corruption, moral or financial has consequences that can be postponed, delayed, though never altogether avoided. War and defeat, also generate circumstances that lead to change. For both—war and defeat—are like a cataclysm, and in the wake of a cataclysm, how can things remain the same? These seeds of the inevitability of change are so often carried in the womb of 'time and circumstance' itself. In the present instance the consequence, the resultant plant, turned out to be 'communist', because in that period and time, the two strongest, both reformist but totally antagonistic ideas that were sweeping the world were fascism and communism. In the Russian context the cataclysm was the First Great War. The incredible stoicism of the Russian peasants in that war, their superstitious fatalism, veneration of the Czar, and their capacity to endure unbelievable privations are legendary as was witnessed in the Brussilov* offensive, then successively, in the Russian army under the Czar, under Kerensky and finally under the Bolsheviks, without boots or rifles, with only a third of them having both! The aftermath of defeat, resultant anarchy and loss of national ethos provided the needed catalyst of 'time and circumstance'. A change was then inevitable, this took the form of a 'socialist revolution', and that became 'historical'. My additional quest, however, at the moment, is to try and understand what has been achieved, by whom and at what cost in this 'revolution'? And what of this mix of Marxism and Islam?

This 'by whom' is significant. To my mind, the existing social order in the USSR is as different to the originally pronounced percepts of Socialist thought, as I think Koestler commented a falcon is from a vulture'! the reality of the Soviet state is far different to the myth of the 'purity of Marxist doctrine'. Even if we spend time now in re-examining each of those fixed nodal points, by which the revolution was to be guided what would we learn? To me it appears as if here the very 'magnetic order of things' got destroyed. The compass needle presently has no fixed guide. Besides, the fundamental weakness of the socialist doctrine

---

* Alexei Brussilov was born in Russia in 1853. He was educated at the Imperial Corps of Pages and after joining the Russian Army served in the war against Turkey (1877-78). Promoted to the rank of general in 1906 Brussilov was given command of the Eighth Army on the outbreak of the First World War. Over the next twelve months Brussilov obtained the reputation as Russia's most successful general. In March 1916, Brussilov was given command of the South Western Army Group on the Eastern Front and led the offensive during the summer of 1916. (www.spartacus.schoolnet.co.uk/FWWbrusilov.htm)

is such that these Marxist utopias have always fallen as instant casualties to the whims and paranoid fantasies of single individuals, turning instead into the very antithesis of the dreamt-of Utopias. I had read somewhere that 'communism does not exist anywhere', what does is a 'totally transposed state authoritarianism, a peculiar, fascistic often contradictory and heretically feudal (in its inner and outer form) system of state administration'. This state apparatus is what has replaced ideology. And it is, this faceless, nameless, answerable to none, all-powerful organisation of the state that exists. It is this machine that has achieved whatever is seen as 'development'. The only incentive now is brute and mindless authority, fear and coercion, not the burning flame of conviction in an ideology. The original incentives were so radically different as to make a mockery of the present day assertions of the 'new Czars'. There was, for example, this theory of the 'collective whole' as against the 'individual', who in the interest of the whole must subserviate. There was to be no legal or any other kind of coercion. And as Koestler again observes with acid dipped pen. There was to be no use of force. All in a Socialist state were to happily and voluntarily go and clear the Siberian Taiga and dig canals in Uzbekistan, whilst the colourful illiterates from the desert sat and learnt the Russian Cyrillic script, 'smilingly and ever diligently'. 'The peasants without demur, moved to hand over to the State their lands, their cattle, sheep, grain, everything and smilingly, every morning, they (went) collectively and in step to the fields cheerfully, singing revolutionary songs'! The state was to belong to them and to their brethren the workers, who were to shun 'chauvinisms, adopt international class solidarity (remember 'Workers of the world unite!) and were to have no complaints'. God, of course, was to die. After all, there were already present new Gods, but 'dialectical materialism' had to be worshipped, even if 'blindly, irrationally and unquestioningly', in whatever form manifest in the Kremlin. These Gods would persuade lovingly, in a 'paternal sort of a way; compelling neither by threat of retribution nor by fears of an afterlife hell', to follow the present if the evil of disobedience ever appeared.

With such incentives towards that 'new tomorrow,' the revolution moved, with 'a song on its lips'?

Did it reach! And where did it reach? What then is the reality? The achievements in the material sense, as can be witnessed, are by any standards impressive. It is deeply troubling, however, to analyse the 'myth of the incentives and the reality of the means' by which all this was achieved. For too long now the world has known of the 'medievalist repressive horrors' of this system at work. Whilst no sane observer can possibly dispute the obvious might of the Soviet state system, every free human being would be shaken to the core in attempting to tabulate the cost in 'human terms' that has had to be paid for all this. It is not just the physical elimination of opponents, or of the incredible suffering of the peasants following upon collectivisations, nor of the continuing blot of Siberian incarcerations either; it is in reality the continuing price that has to be paid, just to keep the 'system going'.

P.S.

Eighteen years after I first came here, I went back to Tashkent. Earlier I was a footloose traveller, wandering with just a backpack, well almost, and then travelled through these enchanted, (then much more closed, too, being Soviet) lands. I am here now as a 'have'; then I was just another arrival, a statistic; today I was received with some ceremony and protocol.

It is the same flight that had easlier taken me out of Delhi, almost straight north; on this occasion too, it was an Ilushyin of the Soviet variety and some vintage, but what a transformation! The plane was full of Indian passengers, some stray European tourists and not one Russian—so sad!

The very same mountains—the Hindukush particularly, at this time of the year covered by dazzling snowfields, and then a short while later there they were: the Tien Shan. The spring crop was yet to be taken; the fields were lush, still green. The land appeared, perhaps because of the ripening crop so much more fertile—much less of a desert. And all the while I wondered where dear Usmanov Egitaly was and what he now did? But I had not the courage to ask.

Samarkand

THE FOUR MAIN OASES IN UZBEKISTAN ARE BOKHARA, FERGHANA, Samarkand and Tashkent. Civilisations have flourished around these sources of water, and it is to these oases that I was headed, as also to Khiva.

There is the usual feeling of being a captive of Russian bureaucracy as I wait and wait and wait in an empty lounge for somebody to come and escort me to the aircraft. l am forbidden from doing so on my own. In fact from doing almost anything by myself. A soft dawn and a clear blue sky; grape vines and Chinar....

In solitary splendour, I am escorted to a battered looking propeller driven aircraft. People walk on the top of its frame. Heavy crates are being loaded with an uncaring 'heaviness'—'drag and dump and thud'!. I wince inwardly every time l hear that sound. I begin to wonder if I am the only passenger that this aircraft is meant to take. Then in a sudden rush it fills up. The Turkic-Mongol have arrived. An old woman, uncompromisingly costumed as of old, complains fearlessly about something and the whole planeload laughs. The hostess a fine, strapping example of Soviet womanhood makes a long-winded announcement about something in Uzbek. We taxi and wait. Almost every minute, or perhaps even less, a plane lands or takes off from the airport. It is full of all kinds of civilian aircraft.

The Shah-i Zinda in Samarkand

We rumble down the runway bumping on its uneven surface, but finally we are airborne, sluggishly though, with the aircraft groaning as if it were heavily pregnant. From the air, at first, seemingly endless squares of green, a fine tracery of irrigation channels, so like life sustaining veins I think. This is truly a remarkable achievement. Two things have simultaneously been achieved: communalisation of land ownership in a region which is still essentially traditional, and this spread of irrigation. Every available inch of the land appears to have been put to use. There are, from the air, clearly visible the distinct, dividing lines between the irrigated and the unirrigated portions of land. Obviously, there is dry cropping, too. Where 'Sovietisation' is not complete there lies the desert which at least from the air appears entirely unchanged, the villages retaining their mud colours of old. But such irrigation is, by any standards, a stupendous feat. The land tracts are of the right economical size, too. As for efficiency and the needed zeal to cultivate someone else's land, even if that 'someone else' be 'Mother Russia'; that alas! is simply not there. Why else should food shortages still plague this land? Or is it perhaps on account of this misplaced emphasis, in Uzbekistan, on cotton?

The air in Samarkand is so much clearer. The atmosphere refreshingly light. Without any doubt a far more agreeable city... Samarkand is old, Alexander and Changez and Taimur and Babur,

The Shah-i Zinda in Samarkand

all have been here, so many strands of history tie this region with India.

The people here are a curious mix of so many influences, of so many conquerors, such a conglomerate; so many of these races are there in Samarkand's airport lounge where all Intourist officials are glued to the T.V., that ubiquitous agent of imbecility. In the hotel the staff is far more friendly than at Tashkent. I observed, when being driven from the airport, citizens of Samarkand at their ease. This ability to squat on the haunches, in the cool shade of a Chinar—or for that matter any where, is as incomparably 'Asian' as you can find. I test (cruelly I think, later) the system for venality. The housekeeper is ready to do my laundry for two roubles. A frightful price to pay in my present indigent state—but I am so delighted to obtain any private service that I pay the amount. In so many indefinable ways, the obliterating stamp of this 'ism' of Marx is not that deeply rooted after all. The driver of the car assigned to me, a Tajik from Bokhara, has that instinctive feudal attitude of deference

The imposing Shah-i Zinda in Samarkand

to authority and to one's superiors. The waiters in the restaurant are also that much more willing to serve and to do so cheerfully.

Samarkand has character, the distinct stamp of a personality, an ancient soul. It appears of a piece, balanced and integrated between its past and its present, achieving this poise only because it accepts the present and atleast, in part, lives in the past.

In Samarkand, Islam is alive; tradition and religious belief and customs and lifestyles have all not been swamped under the dead weight of a faceless system. Here there are still individuals living, there exist still the imperfection of humanity; flies and poverty and beggars and Central Asian hygiene. And Samarkand is such a fascinating town because of its people, also because of its incomparably beautiful monuments, those rare examples of the great flowering of Islamic architecture, so properitorially mine, for they are a part of my historical inheritance, too. Babur, in his memoirs, is lyrical about this ancient seat: 'Samarkand lies on the edge of the civilized world. To the east are Fergana and Kashghar, to the west Bukhara and Khwarazm, to the north Tashkent and Shahrukhiyya, which are also called Shah and Benakath respectively, and to the south Balkh and Termez....'

'Few cities in the civilized world are as pleasant as Samarkand. It is in the fifth clime, 99° 56' longitude, 40° 40' latitude. Samarkand is the seat of the province, which is Transoxiana. Because it has not been stormed and seized by enemies, Samarkand is called 'balda-i-mahfuza'. Samarkand became

The Ulugbek observatory in Samarkand

Muslim during the time of the caliph Uthman. One of the Companions, Qutham, son of Abbas, went there and his tomb outside the Iron Gate is now called Mazar-i-Shah. Samarkand is supposed to have been built by Alexander. The Moghuls and Turks call it "Semizkand" (Fat City). Temür Beg was the first to make it his capital.'

'The grapes, melons, apples, and pomegranates—indeed all fruits—in Samarkand are excellent, but two types of Samarkand fruit are renowned: the apples and Sahibi grapes. The winter is terribly cold, although the snowfall is not so great as in Kabul. The air is good in the summer but not so good as in Kabul'.

The Bibi Khanum Mosque in Samarkand, Uzbekistan

Babur longed for Kabul all his life, wherever he was. He continues:

'In Samarkand and its suburbs are many of Temür Beg's and Ulughbeg Mirza's buildings and gardens. In the Samarkand citadel, Temür Beg had constructed a large four-story pavilion known as the Kök Saray. It is a superb building. Near the Iron Gate, inside the walls, he had a Friday mosque built of stone. Most of the stonemasons sent from Hindustan worked there. The inscription on the mosque, the Koranic verse, 'And Abraham and Ishmael raised the foundation of the house' etc., is written in script so large that it can be read from nearly a league away. This too is a superb building.'

I sit near my window, which I leave open as inside it is stiflingly hot. Outwardly the manifestations are that of a modern city. Wide streets and traffic lights, and for the benefit of a visiting Czech

Kök Saray

delegation the roof top reverberates to some unbearable sound miscalled music. But this evening, at the hotel entrance, there was also Indian film music being played by somebody. In the various mosques that I visited today, the women devoutly kiss the tombs and the greeting is always 'Salaam Waale-Kum', and the parting a blessing and a prayer: 'Rehmat Khuda'.[37]

In sixty years, Communism has not been able to conquer religious faith, not entirely. Repression did not achieve it. I think the crucial generation is that of now—a more open and freer lot, reared on Rock and T.V. They might lose their original moorings, though their parents have yet not. But then, what will remain? And to what extent are the fears of Islamic revivalism in these Soviet Socialist Republics real? This is certainly not a completely assimilated society. The relics of the Taimurid past are there, infinitely more attractive; and near atavistically, hordes of local tourists are drawn to them.

---

37. 'Rehmat Khuda' means 'May blessings of God be with you'.

That is why there are always fresh flowers on the graves and the mausoleums, but I saw not many crowds around the inevitable Lenin statue, laughable to think of anyone putting flowers there. While ruminating on Islam, and the tenacity of faith, it becomes clear that the Soviet invasion of Afghanistan, amongst other causes, was prompted just as much by the compelling need to strategically protect the Southern Soviet flank as by stopping any ingress of 'unsullied Islam into their under belly'. The mythology of all Abrahamic religions[38] talks of the final struggle between the forces of God and that of Satan. Is there any analogy here somewhere? If there is, then who is what?

In the 'bazaar' of Samarkand, I attempt to photograph an elder—but I am correctly, though politely, refused. I then espy a beggar

being driven away. I photograph him and roundly, he and the women present there curse me. For a moment I apprehend he is going to strike me. I do stand my ground but somewhat irresolutely, the camera hanging uselessly by my side.

The bazaar of Samarkand is a flourishing island of free enterprise, where my guide with a smile explains, 'You can bargain'. Where would we be without that? Melons and fruits and potatoes are shovel loaded! Nearby is a long queue: 'What is that for?' a natural query. 'Oh that is the state store; there you have to queue, and you cannot bargain!' In the 'free

The bazaar of Samarkand

---

38. Abrahamic religion is any of those religions deriving from a common ancient Semitic tradition and traced by their adherents to Abraham ('Father/Leader of many'). This forms a large group of related, largely monotheistic religions, generally held to include Judaism, Christianity, Islam, and the Bahá'i Faith, and comprises about half of the world's religious adherents.

The busy bazaar of Samarkand

enterprise', there is bustle and bargaining but no queue. Many centuries back Babur had written: 'The city of Samarkand is amazingly ornamented. There are excellent bakeries and cook shops. The best paper in the world comes from Samarkand. The water for the paper factories comes from the beautiful Kan-i-Gil meadow, beside which is still water, the Qara Su, which is also called Ab-i-Rahmat. Another product of Samarkand is red velvet, which is exported everywhere'. And then, almost lyrically: 'All round the city are exquisite meadows, including the famous Kan-i-Gil, one league to the east and slightly to the north of the city... The rulers of Samarkand have always made this meadow a protected reserve and come out every year to stay (here) for a month to two'.

'How many children do you have?' my guide enquires hesitantly, as we walk back.

'Two sons.' I answer 'Ah, you are a rich man,' is his instantaneous response; strange how sons are wealth in this communist haven, too—but then in this ancient land of many memories, sons are always 'help', they are additional hands, after all this land was ravaged by Alexander and Changez and Taimur. Sons then were wealth, they are so now.

Later, I ask my new guide, a not easily pronounceable name, Gulcheckra Hamidova, if 'she was married'?

'No, I live with my parents. They are going to arrange it for me.'

'How?' I query inquisitively, though I know well enough how.

'Oh! Some friends will suggest to my parents such and such boy. Then they will go and see and if the boy is of 'good family', then the boy's parents will come'..., a long pause. then sadly 'but there are no good boys in Samarkand...' a longer pause, 'It is very difficult to live with parents. My mother, she sits at the window and waits if I am late after 6 p.m.... they are very...' searching for words, hesitating 'How you say...?' She does not wish to use 'bourgeois'; it has disrespectful connotations—at last, and in relief: 'So traditional.'

It is close to midnight again. I have to leave early, the 'kafila' leaves for Bokhara before day break tomorrow. My lean resources deny me the pleasures of even a glass of wine. Enviously I learn though, from Babur that: 'Throughout Transoxiana no wine is stronger than Bukahara wines. When I first drank in Samarkand, I drank (only) Bukhara wines'. And I do fully agree with that ancient warrior's sentiment: 'Only the drinker knows the pleasure of wine. What enjoyments can the sober have'?

Indeed! What do the sober know?

Bukhara

THAT DAWN IN SAMARKAND HAD THE FEEL OF WOMANLY SOFTNESS. The sky was a deep inky blue dome, sprinkled with an entirely unfamiliar pattern of stars; in the East the faint smudge of a low mountain range gently broke the horizon's regularity of line and a faintly blushing sky reluctantly separated from the nightlong embrace of a still dark earth. More prosaically, heavy trucks had all night thundered along the road which lay just below my hotel window. Not very long back it was so different, I know that as a certainty, for I have lived a different form of it. Then it would have been caravans laden with silk and jade and amber and carpets all setting out in that pre-dawn cool from Samarkand's many serais, for Samarkand was *the* great 'caravan serai' of the silk route. This 'silk road' is still there, it exists, but it is now a cement concrete affair and sadly, it is so empty of adventure and romance and bustle. Walking through it now imagination conjures up visions of what it must have been like at one time, and not very long ago too. Serais and cameleers and horse dealers specialising in seizing instantly the gullible. Sharp dealers in all the riches of the East; gold, the finest of silks and 'pashm'[39] and 'shahtoosh',[40] from Hindustan and Kashmir and precious stones, and medicinal charms and aphrodisiacs from China, too. There must then have been conjurers and magicians and lepers and beggars and dervishes from various lands, itinerant fakirs and also an occasional eccentric traveller. The caravans to Bokhara would then have had to leave at a much earlier hour; when the morning star was only so many fingers' width above the horizon. I live in my mind, (for I have lived it in my land) the accompanying send-off, the inevitable barking of dogs, the shouts of cameleers, and the lugubrious groans of camels being couched, loaded and made to set off. The dogs, of course, still bark and ceaselessly: all night long mongrels had snarled, quarrelled and fought on the streets of Samarkand below my open window. Oddly enough, I found in that a reassuring, homely sound. Babur also describes reaching Samarkand and how his entry was received:

'The people of the city were still asleep.' He writes, 'Shopkeepers looked out of their shops, recognised us, and called down blessings upon us. A little while later, the people got wind and a strange joy and jubilation came over our people and the people of the city. Like mad dogs they stoned and clubbed the Uzbeks…(many) were killed in this fashion….'

'Entering through the gate, I proceeded straight to the madarsa and khanaqah and sat down under the khanaqah arch. Dawn broke to alarms and chaos on all sides. Some of the Lords and shopkeepers came as soon as they received word, joyfully bringing us what food they had on hand and

---

39. In Kashmir, Himalayan mountain goats belong to 'Capra hircus'. The fine wool of them is called 'pashm', which is the Persian word for 'wool'. Pashmina is pashm in its woven form.
40. Shahtoosh is the name given to wool derived from the chiru. The fabric woven from this wool carries the same name and is worn by the fashionable worldwide.

pouring blessings upon our head. After dawn word came that the Uzbeks had fortified themselves between the outer and inner gates at the Iron Gate and were putting up a fight. I immediately got to horse and set out for the Iron Gate. With me were ten, fifteen, twenty men....' Babur overcame this resistance and entered triumphantly: 'For nearly 140 years the capital Samarkand had been in our family. Then came the Uzbeks, the foreign foe from God knows where, and took over. Now the property that had slipped from our hands had been restored by God. The plundered and pillaged kingdom once again entered our domain'.

On this day, however, when I was to leave, it is the sound of revving airplane engines that had broken the morning stillness.

Intourist have been overbooked on this flight. East Germans and Czechs and some others belonging to 'Slavic Sovietism' and a lone Indian.

Bukhara Airport has for me a unique distinction. It has the feel of 'home'—of the airport at Jaisalmer now, or what Jodhpur was earlier. Just outside, as waiting area for passengers, are wooden benches placed in an arbour laden with grapes and figs. It is still

Bukhara Airport

very early in the morning. The arbour is silent and littered with figs and overripe prunes that have fallen over night. Even now as I walk they detach themselves from the laden branches and fall almost soundlessly on the leaf-strewn ground. I have to wait, inevitably. A sleepy eyed boy, tousle haired, comes with a long handled broom and sweeps the path untidily. The grapevines and the orchard are charmingly untended, the orchard overgrown with weed, this adds (for me) greatly to its attractive feel. A cat wanders in from nowhere. Nearby a mongrel appears. Sniffing the air and the ground, the cat crouches instantly. Luckily, instinctive animosities fail to get ignited. It is even now barely seven in the morning but there is already some movement. The roads are all wet from being washed, but on the sidewalks, alas! there still lies litter. I am reassured that it is there; no, not out of any sense of perversity, just 'homely' familiarity.

Intourist hotels are all of the same mould. Concrete structures of deliberate and unmatched ugliness, totally lacking in aesthetic appeal. Perhaps, I overstate. The CPWD monstrosities in India would easily give them a run for their money. The toilet in the room is barely sanitary and all fittings malfunction as if with deliberate malice. The public conveniences are outstanding examples of organised inconvenience, they are unmitigated hell, (one could easily be describing Indian public sector hotels), and are barely functional, in a tinny, wood and tin construction kind of way.

My guide tells me her name is Veneirra. 'Venus,' she explains without being asked, as a matter of fact, and not at all suggestively. It is cruel of me to think as I do when she tells me this. As soon as we are in the car, (the driver is a Tajik by the name of Romozon) she starts her practised speech.

'Bukhara is an ancient city. Archaeologists have already established that it is two thousand five hundred years old. But excavation is still going on and soon we hope to be able to announce that we are now three thousand years old, older than Samarkand.' She stops, triumphant, also to draw breath. Not having any 'fast forward' button, I can only press 'stop'. I demand to be taken to the last Sultan's twentieth century palace, the sixteenth century palace, the bazaar and the old town. Great consternation follows, then immediate, hurried consultations between Veneirra and Romozon take place.

Our old acquaintance, dear and intrepid Mohan Lal, has left descriptions of the Aamir of Bukhara, of around the 1840s: 'though severe, he is religious and just', he says but even Mohan Lal is obliged to admit that 'ambition' had caused the 'Aamir' to 'murder all his brothers and all the chief nobles to secure the throne to himself.. 'Ambitious, and careful, too: his water was brought to him direct from the canal in a sealed container, food in a locked box from the kitchen, both to be tasted in his presence by a servant before he would eat or drink of them'. I, too, would do something similar if I had beheaded all and sundry near me. But let us spend some more time with Mohan Lal and his remarkable travelogue—*From Peshawar to Kabul, Balk and Bukhara*. It was written in the middle of the

Samarkand Mausoleum Gur-e-Amir, Samarkand

nineteenth century, when he accompanied Burnes. Mohan Lal wrote it in English, himself, in a narrative form and style that is remarkable for its lucidity, expressions and observations. For example, he had observed that the Amir then had 'small eyes, in a visage gaunt and pale', but that they never 'activated the malevolence of the brain behind them'. What a truly marvellous sentence, depicting sharply an extremely sinister person with a remarkable economy of expression. Mohan Lal, after a long and arduous journey writes: 'entered this morning, the city of Bukhara, which is encompassed by sandy suburbs. The walls are surrounded by an irregular line of trees, and protected by dry ditches. It is the largest and most populous and wealthy city in the whole region of Tartary. The splendid mosques and magnificent colleges, which are 360 in number, contain students who are unqualified both in the Persian and Arabic languages, but they write a very good hand. The doors of the buildings are covered with filth. Registan, the large bazaar which is roofed, has a very striking appearance. The shops, which succeed each other in a straight line, present a splendid sight. They are ornamented with beautiful Chinaware and Russian bottles, against which hang large but thin pieces of tin. The caravans of Bukhara, which generally consist of four thousand or five thousand camels, loaded with oriental articles, formerly sent to Russia through the road of Khiva, once a year, conveyed their beautiful goods to the rich market of Makria for sale'. The Mullahs of that remote period have praised Bukhara in the following manner:

'Samarkand is the light of the face of the world; Bukhara is the strength of the Islamic faith. If Mashad had not the tomb of Imam Raza, it would be the place of the outcasts in the earth!'

Then, two days later, an early walk led Mohan Lal 'through the bazaar called Sarafan, where he observed two Mohammedans mounted on camels, guarded by four sepoys who had only whips

The Minar-e-Kalian in Bukhara

in their hands. They were ordered to be scourged by the Qazi for not saying their morning prayers, and for sleeping after the sun was up. (Sounds ominously familiar) Some are chastised for smoking, some for drinking, and others for snuffing'. Mohan Lal is endowed, of course, with admirable energy, natural curiosity but also an eye for the beautiful: 'On my return I passed through the famous street of the Jews, where I scarcely saw a man or a woman devoid of beauty. All of them were alluring, and their persons enticing; they were gazing out of the door at those who passed through the street. They are the most delicate of any people I have seen between Delhi and Bukhara. I am sure if any Indian, who is a worshipper of beauty, should come to Bukhara, he would undoubtedly be a victim to the charms of these Jewesses. Their dress is of a curious fashion, calculated to entice the heart of men.' But alas! discrimination proliferated even in the midst of such beauty: 'The Hindus and Jews of Bukhara are not allowed to mount on horseback, and can tie neither turban, cloths, nor shawls round their waist. I was visited by a crowd of

Hindus, who came merely to inquire of me (my) object in making such a long journey.

'He informed that there are about three hundred Hindus in Bukhara, and they live in a caravansary of their own. They are chiefly natives of Shikarpur, in Sind, and their number is on the increase. The Uzbeks and indeed all the Muhammedans find themselves vanquished by the industry of these people who will stake the largest sums of money for the smallest gain.

'Among the Hindus we had a singular visitor in a deserter from the Indian Army at Bombay! He had set out on a pilgrimage to all the shrines of the Hindu world, and was then proceeding to the fire temples on the shores of the Caspian. I knew many of the officers of the Regiment (the 24th N.I.) to which he had belonged, and felt pleased at hearing names, which were familiar to me in this remote city. I listened with interest to the man's detail of his adventures and travels, nor was he deterred by any fear that I would lodge information against him and secure his apprehension. I looked upon him as a brother in arms, and he amused me with many a tale.... This man, when he first showed himself, was disguised in the dress of a pilgrim; but the carriage of a soldier is not to be mistaken, though he has traversed the mountains and deserts to Bukhara'.

From that satchel of school boy memories then reappeared also Stoddard and Connolly and their tragic heroism; but why disturb them again, I thought.

We are there, at the Emir's old palace, the residence of a king, which is not at all like a palace, a much humbler building, comprising a very large and magnificent mosque, painted with numerous colours. The twentieth century palace is stranger still, a mixture of ornate and Czarist Russia and the East. The entrance to it is through a narrow, covered corridor with a sharp bend. Bukhara, even in 1920, when this palace was built, was all of medieval mentality. These bends in entrances were to prevent an enemy from rushing straight in. Massive wooden doors of intricate finery adorned various entrances. Then the verandhas—if there is not a

The Emir's Palace

verandha or courtyard in an Eastern house it is incomplete. Sad, abandoned, beautiful plasterwork such as I have seen so many times, in a similar state of neglect back home. The place of prominence (appropriately enough I suppose in this egalitarian world of 'workers unite' etc.) is given to the main craftsman (not the Sultan) and a drawing of his likeness—one Ustad Ali—is displayed. The park where peacocks, no doubt imported from India roam is now, I am informed by my diligent guide, a kidney sanatorium. 'Our dry climate and water is suitable for this.' I am more interested, however, in the last Sultan, not the state of kidneys of the Soviet citizens today, and therefore continue to enquire about him.

'He fled to Afghanistan with his son and died there, in 1947.' A very terse reply, denoting an abrupt ending to what sounds almost like yesterday. 'His other son is in Russia.' She continued. 'Where?' I persist. 'Oh, Leningrad or somewhere.' This is much too casual. 'What does he do?' Suspicious now, therefore, obstinately persisting.

'He is in the military or something.'

'But what is he in the military? Surely, he must visit here sometimes?'

'No, no he does not visit,' then, 'I do not know,' a tame afterthought.

'But if he is in the military, why Leningrad?'

'Oh, he is a general or something.'

There, I have got what I wanted, rather remarkable that a scion of the feudal order continues in rank and as a general, too.

As we leave this sad reminder of the past, a wedding party arrives: a newly married couple. They are all Tajiks. Most unfortunately to my eyes, they have abandoned their ancient finery and are now dressed in some drab western suit etc., as European Russians would do. The bride is dressed in white, not traditionally, but she does like a proper Muslim bride, remain deferential and does not raise her head. The groom is in a dull unimaginative dark suit. But I am both intrigued and fascinated by this adherence to an ancient feudal custom. No doubt newly weds, until well into this century, presented themselves to the Emir, for his blessings, or for letting the feudal's lascivious claims assert their privilege, as a 'right', before the groom could establish any of his marital variety.

'But why are they here now?' I ask without sharing any of the preceding thoughts, of course. 'Oh', she starts all her sentences with this exclamation, 'Oh, young couples like to be photographed here. It is such a beautiful place.'

The old palace is really a fort. A sixteenth century mud structure rising in the middle of the town. Somewhat of a mixture between Jaisalmer and Lathi. The inside of it is dominated by a spectacular courtyard of Roman proportions. All around runs a raised parapet, on the northern end of which stands a wooden awning, supported by tall wooden pillars, intricately carved. In the well of the courtyard are cobbled stones. But the courtyard itself is open to a bright and brilliant blue sky. This is the main assembly area. I imagine the romance and colour of an earlier gathering here, when the courtyard would be laid with carpets of several hues and intricate weave; and

A wedding in Bukhara

when all around the parapet would sit Khans and chieftains from the desert, and under this canopy, the inheritor of the ancient Sultanate of Bukhara—so cruel, uncaring and tyrannical, but also so far from everywhere.

Going down, I find tiny cubicles for incarcerating the infidels and the vagrants; my guide, too, points them out. I enquire if such things happen now? In the tense verbiage of the reply, learnt by rote, the point of my question is lost.

I turn to have a last look at this magnificent sight. Down the fort gateway are coming some Tajiks dressed as of old. I greet them. They enquire of my guide where I am from? 'Hindustan.' She informs. I repeat their 'assalum a malik,' appropriately, and add a Samarkandi 'Rehmat-i-Khuda.' The old man lets out a prolonged sigh, full of atavistic longing, expressing unspokenly so many sentiments, perhaps also that even to hear such greetings again is a wonder. I too wonder? He must imagine that coming from Hindustan I am a Muslim; and

Courtyard in the Old Palace

for his sake, at that moment, I wished I did not have to disappoint him.

The mosques and the madarsas and the great tombs, Islam has without doubt given birth to one of the most prolific and impressive schools of architecture—from the moorish influences in the Iberian Peninsula, along both sides of the Mediterranean, stretching as far East as India. There is for instance—the 'Chasm e Ayab'—a communist interpretation of which is 'Job' and how the 'clergy' they say continuously fooled' the citizens, by calling the miraculous waters of this well as a 'gift of God'. 'What else are they?' I enquire. Dialectical materialism replies: 'Minerals and salts': But 'from where have come these?' All this feels like peeling layers of onionskin, endlessly.

The old town of Bukhara has alleys and lanes so familiar to my Indian eyes. Open gutters and hordes of children playing barefoot and two kites lazily circling in a cerrulean sky. The houses are plastered with a mixture of clay and straw. The effect is to turn them the

A view of the amphitheatre in the Old Palace

same colour as the 'Kizil Kum', the 'red sand desert' which surrounds Bukhara, except that the name of the desert is so obviously a misnomer for the sand is not red — it is plain clay colour. Round domes; a multiple proliferation of them, each built, I suppose, by some devout citizen to earn merit. Women squat outside their houses for air and routinely yell at truant children. This squatting posture again, is without doubt, the posture of infinite patience—only Asians and the Africans have it.

Part of the old town is the market place, alongside which runs an open canal of the same period. Then more mosques and madarasas. An old woman sits by the mosque wall and on the ground in front spreads her wares to sell. The tradition of the bazaar dies hard. The sweeping arm of reform has succeeded in shutting this ancient bazaar; as old as Bukhara. But what can Bukhara be without its trade? The 'Bukhara carpets' came actually from Turkemania, or even further away but because they were traded here they acquired this eponymous title. The oasis around

The imposing entrance to the Bukhara ark citadel

which this town developed comes at the end of the river 'Zaval Shams'—'Gold carrying'. It carried no gold, never did. The symbolism of the name lay in the gold which came with the trade and the routes of commerce that lay along this river. That certainly carried gold.

Because the new bazaar is a parody of the old, private trade arrives in wheel barrows. Privately grown vegetables and fruit and honey find their way here. The donkeys of old are gone, almost, and in their place has come the 'modern' wheel barrow. (In the display section of the fort there is a plough, still in use with us in India, wooden, and in a shape as old as mankind. The guide pointed it out to me as 'a primitive agricultural instrument'!

'Why primitive?' I enquired with pointed sharpness.

'Because it was used by the primitive man.' Thereafter, I could not find a sharp enough retort and neither could I very well say. 'We use it in India and we are not primitive, and I have used it, too.'

Anyway, to come back to the new bazaar: covered sheds; state capitalism and private enterprise distinguished only by the presence of queues in one and their absence in the other. In the background the old city wall, entirely of mud, and now disintegrating at places. In one corner of the shed, meat carcasses and a slow queue. The butcher's assistant, (there was one) hacking the great big limbs of the carcass with an axe, swinging it up, as if chopping wood, and with a great thud heavily he … comes down. Flies then rise in a dark cloud—to me, in this communist utopia, they

A village near Bukhara

appear as cheeky by their mere presence. The state preserves its enterprise by putting it inside a shed. The private variety cheerfully braves the elements outside and judging by their respective demeanour seems to cope not at all badly.

Night has fallen in this ancient oasis of Bukhara. A clear desert sky. Underneath lies today's city with electric lights. The past clings, however, in the sights and sounds; the barking of dogs in the dark of the night; (the sight of a shepherd early this morning), the desert air has by now cooled. So what is the final tally? A stupendous achievement if one counts the modernisation, the tarmac roads and traffic lights, and imposing administrative buildings and all the lowly Intourist officials, sitting self-importantly in their air-conditioned offices. People appear to be well-fed and reasonably, if tastelessly clothed, and obviously there is a roof for all. This is a great achievement

Bazaar in Tashkent

by any reckoning. To be able to make an effective dent in the accumulated silt of human destitution; to feed, to clothe and to house. Any administrative machinery effective enough to be able to achieve all this has met with the primary requirements. But is the philosophy behind governance to merely engineer an administratively effective instrument? And what happens then to the spiritual? What happens to dreams and aspirations and myths and wonderment of human kind?

I do not think old Bukhara has all died. I am sure it lives—some where out there in the 'Kizil Kum', and here in the hearts of the Tajiks and Uzbeks. This evening I went to see what I was told is 'our traditional concert'. I was driven there in a Russian bus, wildly careering around corners and bullying all others on the road aside. In an old 'madarsa', the caricatures which go by the name 'folk art' perform their drill. A saddening performance. They are all spruced up, dressed alike, not different from our 'official tribals', for the Republic Day parades. The dancers are in Russian ballet shoes and musicians in shirts and 'ties' of the official issue variety, and all in exactly alike Uzbek 'phirans' on top. Sounds, rhythms and forms

Chashma ayab mausoleum

so akin to Kashmir. One poor girl is made to ape a belly dance—why this monstrosity in Uzbekistan? I wonder, but worse, is a 'censored' version of it. And in this 'belly dance' to make her actually cover her belly! (The singers sang patriotic songs about 'workers unity', and 'peace', and such other 'noble themes') Where, one wonders, are the 'real songs' of this land? It is the land of the nomad that has been grazed barren and treeless by the passage of countless centuries of herdsman. This is not the song, the dance, the celebrations or the colour of Bukhara.

I have no doubts, the roots of Bukhara will continue to drink deep in the Chasm-e-Ayub and Zamal Sham; one for faith and cure, the other for Gold.

'The unbelievable epochs are the cradles of new superstitions'.

– Amiel

Ferghana

HAD I BEEN ABLE TO TRAVEL TO FERGHANA BY ROAD AND IN slow stages, this veil over the unseen face of today's Uzbekistan, yesterdays Sogdiana, would certainly have lifted. I was told, when finally I got permission even to travel to Ferghana, that I should not ask for more or I else might lose even this opening. A small aircraft flew us to this ancient seat of Babur's.

The bare, denuded lower reaches of Tien Shan are the first to be sighted. Grazed dry to the primeval colour of earth by centuries of nomadic herdsman, not a tree to be seen. The aircraft twists and turns in one direction first then in the other, and turns yet again— I wonder why? Is this because we are so close to that ancient 'knot': the 'Hindu-Kush'? Continents and civilisations and strategic imperatives have got knotted here for as long as man can remember. But then, at a more mundane level, Kashghar and the Panjshir are only some minutes of flying error away.

The USSR invaded Afghanistan because they assessed that this land was an absolutely vitally needed extension of their imperial interests. They could simply not have let an aggressively Islamic Afghanistan exist; that would threaten all Asia, so they reckoned. The challenge lay in assessing correctly the proper time for such a venture, also an exploitable opportunity. It is again this very central strategic imperative that had persuaded Russia earlier, subsequently the USSR to assimilate Uzbekistan in the Soviet Empire itself. Just one brief visit to this Islamic heartland of the USSR is enough to further cement such convictions. Besides, what on earth was India doing all these years? Our thinkers and planners and our governments ought to have seen this coming long back, for if we in India could not (or did not) assess what was happening in Afghanistan then that is truly worrisome! Am I then in error to write and say that in 'two or three years' the Russian position in Afghanistan will become untenable? Even though Afghanistan remains vital for them, not so much for the oils of West Asia, or the so called 'warm water ports' or such other stretched theories, but simply for securing the Soviet Union's southern Islamic underbelly. The Ayatollah revolution of Islamic fundamentalism in Iran has further heightened their apprehensions, not the governing inadequacies of Noor Mohd. Tarakki, or Hafizullah Amin or Babrak Karmal.

These lands of Central Asia are the deep hinterland of Islam, the incredible, geographic sweep of the proselytising sword of Islam. Faith in Islam lives here, perhaps dormant and silent and sub-surface at present, but still as a vital, living force; confused-yes, by this onslaught of dialectical materialism, but fearfully existing even if as but atavistic gropings, the usual mixture of superstition and custom and social norms. And even sixty years after the 'Great Revolution', this fountain of Islam has not dried up. This too, is a great failure of this Communist regime. Like Islam here, so in USSR, so too Buddhism in Tibet. But can Islam, does Islam share state power with other faiths? No, not really. 'Dar-ul-Rab', the 'land of God' is possible only with Islamic jurisprudence, Islamic governance and with the rule of the Sharia, interpreted and administered by the faithful alone.

NOTES FROM MY DIARY

Tien Shan and Pamirs, late reception, 'Usmanov Egitaly', guide, Uzbek, Salaries, costs of living, Housing, Bazaar, (Jews, Karakuli)/ stories, systems, Racism, Department store, Uzbek Tea Houses, 'Usmanov an orphan', 5 children, apartment life, Visit Margileh, purchases in bazaar, friendlier Uzbeks, presents, visiting homes, horses, Women carrying grass on head, private cows, boys in canal swimming, Discussion of an Afghan host and dinner, Russian predominance, this cultural benumbing by 'Rock',

Salary 150 Rbls (3 shoes, 75 Km by car, one dress)

Apartments 12—15 Rbls (Gas+Water, no electricity)

Rice: Govt. 30 Kopeks/Kg, Private 4-5 Rbls.

Meat: Govt. 1.30—1.90 Rbls/kg, Private 5—9 Rbls

The absence of a vast number of young,—where are they military duty?

'Like giant hawks with their skull caps fitted on.'

The hotel where I was lodged had no dining room. For meals I had to walk, not too great a distance though, to a restaurant. I did not know where it was or in what direction to search. But the absence of language is never really such a barrier. I employ sign language about eating and that suffices most of the time. On the sidewalk, at that time of the evening, as in any self-respecting Asian city worth its salt, there were present any number of idle bystanders, sitting, yawning, gaping, gossiping or just taking the evening air. With that disarming and spontaneous generosity of the idle, a number of them volunteered to escort me all the way to the restaurant. In consequence, conversation was uninterruptedly multilingual, with nobody understanding what I was saying or I what they were conveying, yet grasping broadly the trend of it. I use Hindi, Urdu, and a smattering of Farsi, English; answers flow from all sides in Uzbek or Russian. An Afghan claims the right of 'ownership' over me, as being entitled to take care of me. He comes and sits with me on the table, orders a bottle of wine. Upon my offering to share, he breaks a minuscule bit of symbolic bread with me. He cannot understand what I am saying and, as earlier what he is. I catch the names 'Jalalabad', 'Lahore', 'Thakur' (presumably for 'Rabindra Nath'), 'Prem Chand', 'Kishan Chand' etc. I am astonished genuinely, and say so. The sentiments of life, praise, love, hate, passion, violence can do without the coarse instrumentality of language; these sentiments belong to a repertoire that is global. Easy, therefore he 'understands' whatever I say.

'Hindustan many million Musulman?' It is a question, an affirmation, and a statement also of kinship, all this in one go.

'"Roos"(For Russia) many million Musulman—No masjid?,' I remind him. He rolls his eyes half fearfully, half in agreement, as if to even suggest a disagreement would be like heresy.

'Namaz?' I query. A pious look comes upon his face and he recites the opening Surra; here in a strange eating house in Soviet controlled Central Asian Ferghana, where the style and decor and everything else has been imported from a different and distant European Commissar's unimaginative mind, to hear those lines of faith... there is not much that was left to be said after that. My question had put him in a mood of gloomy introspection. He borrows and smokes a few more of my cigarettes, and then in one of those unbelievable acts of spontaneous generosity (which, repeatedly I have witnessed, but which only Asians so easily demonstrate) goes in and pays for my meal, wine etc. etc. I protest vehemently, take out my money, then am weakened in my protests because I realise how rude it must seem, this attempt to repay an emotion. We exchange slips of paper with respective addresses. On the pavement we embrace. 'Hindu—Afghan Bhai Bhai.' I am relieved. The Russian custom is to kiss on the lips.

I have taught the housekeepers on the floor to give me tea whenever I call. They are all such dears, all pensioners, uncomfortably fat, uniformly forbidding in appearance and unvaryingly lonely— but all, eventually, femininely soft.

A smile followed by 'Chai?' as both a query and a plea.

The first response is a gruff 'Nyet.'

I pretend she means 'Yes', and launch into all the 'thank you' words that I know of, can think of, liberally interspersed with all the Russian I am able to muster.

A resigned, exasperated shaking of the head, then finally the woman in her takes over.

Tea follows.

But all this really began with the flight that brought me here. The aircraft crosses the craggy denuded hills and the desert sands spread out below. The very first warnings of the approaching range of mountains are masses, bank upon bank of clouds. For days there has not been seen a single cloud in the sky—not even of the size of a flyspeck. What has caused this sudden manifestation are the mountains: Magnificently, toweringly, piercing the clouds, emerge the mighty Pamirs—snow clad, ordinarily hidden by cloud banks, unknown, and mysterious. Revealed now as if a great, secret mood had suddenly unfolded. What cataclysms of celestial origins have tied these mighty mountain chains into this ancient and hoary 'Kush' (knot) of the Hindus? It is here that the 'Hindu Kush' range also lies. And beyond them, their gleaming peaks, to their south, lies that fabled land of 'Hind', my land. I wonder if somewhere in his adolescent mind it was on this vision that Babur had dwelt—wondering, dreaming, aspiring to conquer that fabled Hind.

'The province of Fergana is in the fifth clime', Babur wrote later in his memoirs, 'situated on the edge of the civilized world. To the east is Kashghar, to the west Samarkand and to the south the mountains that border Badakhshan. To the north, although formerly there were cities like Almalyk, Almatu, and Yangi which is called Otrar in books because the Moghuls and Uzbeks passed there, there (now) is no longer any civilisation'.

He informs that 'It is a smallish province'. (Ferghana) 'Grain and fruit are plentiful. All around are mountains, except on the western side, that is, in Samarkand and Khodzhent, where there are none. So, aside from that direction, foreign enemies cannot penetrate'.

These memoirs are a treasure house of information. We come to learn from Babur that: there are seven towns in Ferghana.... Of the towns on the southern side, one is Andizhan, the capital of Ferghana, located in the middle of the province. Grain and fruit are plentiful there, and the melons and grapes are excellent. During the melon season in the fall it is customary not even to sell them at the melon patches, no pears are better than those from Andizhan. In all of Transoxiana, after the Samarkand and Kish fortresses, no fortress is larger than that in Andizhan.... Game and sporting birds are also plentiful in Andizhan. The pheasants get extremely fat and it is said that not even four people can finish eating a stew made from just one. The saying goes, 'Apples of Samarkand and pomegranates of Khodzhent. Today, however, the pomegranates from Margilan are much better....' Marvellously anecdotal *Baburnama* combines information with wit: 'Between Khodzhent and Kanibadam is a desert wilderness called Ha Darwesh. There, a fierce wind always blows east toward Margilan and west to Khodzhent. It is said that several dervishes encountered the wind there and, unable to find each other, cried out, 'Hey, dervish!' over and over until they all perished. From that time, the place has been called Ha Darwesh'.

Our aircraft begins its descent, finally lands, and what a let down! An execration of an industrial area scars the fair face of this fabled valley of Ferghana. Chimneys, smoke, industrial yards—black, menacing and indescribably ugly. The system failed yet again, only temporarily though. There was no one at the airport, no Intourist guide, no car, no interpreter. Being quite an old hand at all this by now, I made a 'show'—I went and stood in the middle of the airport departure lounge meant only for 'natives'. I knew they will have to take notice and that I have to say no more than 'Intourist' and 'Indian'. Someone asks me for my passport. I refuse to understand. I certainly am not parting with that—no, not that. So there I am, a queer bird in the middle of this milling confusion, which most Russian departure lounges in any event are. The counters are all mobbed by anxious crowds, all clutching documents of identity—

(man/woman reduced to 'paper', recognisable only if that 'paper' is present, that, too, all duly stamped—for without a proper stamp even 'paper' is not 'paper' and all this always in duplicate too; so many multiple 'cates'—where does it all end up?) Occasionally, a name is called and there is suddenly an immediate but frantic agitation in that congealed mass. I am sure a great deal of influence pedalling must go on to obtain the scarce seats on Russia's internal airlines; quite like back home, I conclude ruefully. My presence adds to the confusion. A police look-alike functionary (the same who had asked for my passport), totally unused to being talked back to, leave alone such rank disobedience, had to be further defeated by the barrier of language, with which I had effectively cloaked all my 'non-violent non-cooperation', all these refusals uptil now. Finally, the functionary gave up, then talked to someone. Suddenly a number of telephones were jangling busily; frantic calls were in the air. A functionary of the airlines detached himself from the check-in-counter, (leaving all the 'paper-possessing' citizens waiting, stranded. How they must curse me at this moment, I think) and motions me to follow. He commands somebody who rushes and unloads my bags, until then lying in the aircraft. Then suddenly appears: laughing, cheerful, not in the least bit remorseful at being late, my guide and interpreter for the next few days; Usmanov Egitaly, an Uzbek. The first (Usmanov) a patronymic, the second (Egitaly) his own.

UE is fair with dark hair and only faintly Mongoloid features. A developing paunch indicates his easygoing, carefree and open nature and his fondness for eating. We hit it off instantly. I laugh at the insincerity of his apologies about being late. He laughs back, knowingly. Volunteering to pick up my baggage, but only half-heartedly, he then commands someone else to do it, and is actually obeyed—not with any surly reluctance, not, too, as if the orders came from a barely tolerated, but otherwise loathsome superior, this ready compliance was to meet the wishes of someone liked, to please him.

'Mr. Singh, welcome to Ferghana; you are the first Indian to ever visit this town as a tourist.' UE had made amends for his unpunctuality, cleverly employing flattery.

That information about my being 'the first', true or false, had made my day. We discuss programmes. I express a desire to see Babur's birthplace.

'That is Andijan, not open to tourists; but also no monuments there, nothing. Just a town of buildings.'

I have not the heart to tell him that all towns have buildings, or counter his views by sharing Babur's writings about Andizhan—'no pears are better'; no 'fortress larger'.

'Well then, perhaps Kokand,' I am disappointed but not overmuch, it was a long shot in any case.

'That will cost you money,' informs UE, the practical Uzbek civil servant and functionary that he is.

'But I do have a voucher for it.' I remonstrate, momentary spasms about shortage of money, about the budgetary tightness of my purse, etc. arresting me.

'Ha, Ha, Ha, then it will not cost you money,' says UE. In the Indian Military Academy, when there as a 'Gentleman (I presume) Cadet', I had learnt a stock phrase for this kind of carefreeness—'couldn't-care-less', it was called, and that is what UE has in plenty.

On the sightseeing tour, he directs the driver to take us into the centre of the town and has the car parked under the cool shade of a Chinar.

'This is our latest cinema hall,' he says, watching my face intently. I am not even looking, because patently this does not interest me at all, this latest wonder of the Soviet (tenth or twelfth or how so ever many) five year plans. UE knows that.

'Mr. Singh, sometimes it is better to see with eyes, not hear with ear!' UE is lazy but he is nothing if not shrewd, and he has a fine turn of phrase. But then, it is well enough known that the intelligent but lazy make the best officers; it is the dull and the hard working lot that are always the greatest menace. After all, it is tiresome to be going on endlessly about socialism, and that, too, in this enervating heat of Ferghana, at three in a Central Asian summer afternoon.

'What we shall do? What you want to see?' UE enquires, even the colloquialism could be Indian.

'I want to see people, Egitaly, meet people in their homes; human beings, not cement concrete buildings.'

He is thoughtful, then answers hesitantly, 'How you say—in private homes, people shy. You know my home, you are welcome, you are my guest. (This by placing the palm of his hand on his heart.)' He means it too, that is patent. I save him of this embarrassment.

'Married, Egitaly?'

'Yes, five children,' both proud and somewhat shy.

'How much salary do you get?'

'Not enough,' UE, 'for I have five children,' he adds as explanation.

'How much is 'not enough'?' I persist.

'150 Roubles?' UE.

'What can you buy for 150 Roubles?'

'Not much, not much,' he laughs at me, with me, from his belly, then continues, 'you can buy three pairs of plastic shoes, or one trouser and a shirt, or go seventy-five kilometres in this car.'

'What about food, you have young children?' I ask.

'Food? No food—Ha Ha Ha.'

'Is food expensive to buy?'

'Expensive? Yes. In government shop not, but also in quality—no.'

'What about meat?'

'Meat? Have you seen meat in shop anywhere?' he answers by this 'tell-all' query.

'How much does meat cost?'

'In government shop Rbl 1.30 to 1.90 per kg, but not there. In private shop Rbls 5.90 per kg for sheep, 5.30 for cow.' UE.

'What? Are there private shops?'

'Farmers from outside town, with private houses, some land, some sheep, some cow. They come and sell.'

My friendly guide, Egitaly Usmanov (Right)

'You can get anything from private shop?'

'Yes anything, all good quality, you can bargain. In government shop poor quality, no bargain.' By then, through a tacit, unstated agreement we have headed straight for the bazaar where Egitaly has to make same purchases for which he says he gets no time and where, he further informs me with a laugh: 'You will see life—Uzbeks. Plenty Uzbek girls, but only *to* see, not touch. Ha, Ha, against law!'

'Look at this rice,' he is now buying rice from a private vendor who has, thoughtfully, opened his stall just outside the government shop. This truly is private enterprise, for those that want rice will come here, and if this rice does not match what is supplied by the government, well then, clearly he would fail. Egitaly buys from the private vendor.

'What is the difference in price?' I enquire.

'Government shop thirty kopek per kg; private, four roubles and thirty kopek! But look at this rice,' and irreverently he picks up a

Inside an Uzbek Bazaar
Ferghana

fistful from the government stock, in the face of the indifferent government appointed shop tender who clearly has more paper work to attend to than rice to sell. Also judging from the multitude of forms and price tags and notice boards, all this could so easily be a ration shop back home.

'Do all Russian towns have bazaars?' I am fascinated by the man and the theme of private enterprise, struggling and to all appearances, succeeding.

'Yes,' emphatically. 'All, but European bazaars are not as interesting as ours.' Dear UE is a man of discernment.

'Do you have racial problems?'

'You mean marriage between different nationalities?'

'Yes.'

'Ha Ha, parents don't like. Russian girls sometime marry Uzbek, but Uzbek girl, Russian man—no.'

I have persuaded him to take me to an Uzbek teahouse. There are plenty of them. Each Chinar shaded square has them: 'You see we have samosa, pulao, just like you.' I point to the number of old men sitting in these shops, in the cool of the shade. Egitaly picks up the thread again.

'Yes, they all sit and talk of when they were this high (Lowers his hand to knee height) and how good things then were, and how the young now are no good. It is the traditional way of wasting time. Ha, Ha, meet in a 'chai khana' in the afternoon and talk, Ha, Ha.'

We are going past a block of flats and I enquire of Egitaly where he lives.

A Chai Khana, frequented by all

'In one these, it is a house but not home. I have four room apartment. I was orphan. My grandmother bring me up. Then I live in hostel. Then I get scholarship. You don't get it if you fail—Ha! Ha! Ha. Then I marry, large family, we have four rooms. But in summer, it very hot, forty-three degrees! It is not home. For home you need land, you need garden, some grapes, you know—for shade and for children to play under and to sometime to eat....' He pauses, then with impeccable fairness and possibly because reminded of his orphaned childhood, adds poignantly 'But this house better if you have nowhere to go—No House...' Egitaly is now a shade less exuberant but is not sentimental.

I readily agree but only through an assenting and understanding silence.

We pass a kiosk inside which sits a cobbler. Enroute, we had passed a large government owned department store, looking at which Egitaly with acute perception and not without humour had said, 'But this you do not want to see?' both a question and a statement. I laughed out my agreement. Seeing the cobbler I asked about the trade.

'Most of them Jews. Some from Bokhara. You know why Jews cobblers? Because they roam so much, Egypt and Iran and Arabia, then they decide to do all trade, so cobbler. You know Emir of Bukhara—the last Emir, he have many Jews and many girls from India and Persia and many Negro. You know why we call Kara-Kul, it mean 'black curl', like Negro hair, so the Cap Kara-Kul, tight hair. Jews speak Persian in Ferghana. If they go to Israel, they thrown out.' There is venom in his voice. What is it? An inherited prejudice, anti-Semitism, or is it the anger of the Soviet state against Jewish immigration to their 'homeland' that is being reflected?

During the course of the conversation, I have told Egitaly about my politics and that I am also a farmer (of sorts) and the extent of my land.

'Your sons, they work with you on the farm?' UE asks a very good question.

I am somewhat embarrassed answering 'No, they are at school.'

'Then your wife?'

'Yes, she does some work, but then there are others, too.'

'You employ people to work for you?'

'Yes,' I feel I need to explain. 'Look Egitaly, they work to help me on the farm and I pay them wages.'

'Oh! You do not have to explain, Mr. Singh, you know a lot of things. You have seen world. I have not but I know. All systems have: some work, others command. With us you become Farm Director...(a long pause).' He does not go on. But he starts on another theme, 'You know all town people eat, eat, eat. Only villagers produce, produce. No? Why?'

It hardly needs answer. He knows it already. Not for nothing has UE, a child orphaned when three years old, come up to be what he is.

'But in India, Mr. Singh you have great, how you say, poor.'

Yes, Egitaly, sadly yes. And that is the fundamental dilemma—which is the worst hell? Villages without medicine, septic childbeds, grinding poverty, benumbing hunger, shelterless humans, but free, and this other, an oppressive, soulless, mindless state apparatus and the crushing heel of the Commissar, but houses which are not 'homes', and queues to nowhere—one misery for another?

I have written for far too long, it is 1.45 a.m. I forgot the watch or to look at it—the mind speaks and the pen follows. Later today, I go to Kokand.

Kokand

THOUGH KOKAND IS JUST ABOUT HUNDRED KILOMETERS OR SO from Ferghana, thankfully I could travel to it only by road. In its time this was a great and a sprawling Khanate: the Kokand Khanate. Now that ancient splendour is all gone, and Kokand has been reduced to a Europeanised, centralised, 'township and that too of no great distinction', a 'progressive', Soviet township. But that description, though accurate, omits achievements altogether. This land, at one time an outpost of the Czarist Empire and a mix of medieval Khanates, Sultanates and Emirates, has through an enormously costly effort (in all respects) of the Soviet apparatus, now been lifted out of poverty and shoved forcibly into the twentieth century. The achievements in material terms are impressive. The effort that has gone into it, difficult to measure—equally, the costs, it is so apparent, have been staggering in human terms, in cultural terms, in psychological terms. On this very 'Asian' of Asian lands, has got transplanted a Communist Europeanisation. Whether this graft has truly or will ever firmly take root is patently an open question.

Take religion. Soon after the Great Revolution, by decree, religion was abolished. God was declared as having died, as non-existent, a myth, as total 'superstition'. Through the length and breadth of Uzbekistan, mosques were boarded up, the muezzein fell silent, their call which had for centuries echoed across the sands, was not heard any more. It is difficult after all to disobey the might of a Commissar's decree, he is there, present all the time, but it is immensely more difficult to dig out from the inner-most recesses and depths of mankind's sub-conscious these deep roots of faith. For all religions, at a certain level of original observance, did also give birth to a social order of, rather in the land, and even the daily ritual of the faithful. In traditional societies far more so, because there not only did personal observances flow directly from religious decrees, but religion from its roots of spirituality also gave to humankind that vital life sustaining resource: a sense of the mystique of life, a consciousness about the Divine, an acceptance of the finiteness of living, of the end of life. Communism did not ever find an answer to that greatest of all questions: 'What is death? Why death'? What for all this, then? All religions address this question, in different ways of course, coming up with different answers; but for human beings there is some solace in that, for religion is a comfort against that finality, of the end of life. Communists did not answer that, ever, but they too will meet the tireless reaper someday.

6 AUG : Kokand : Notes

Drive, Tea House, Egitaly on speed limits, Tea House visitor enquiring about 'rich' in India, talk an elections in India and USSR, cheating in both, kinds, 99.9% vote, 'elected before elections, Afghanistan and Poland, violence of reaction to 'take, take from USSR' etc, e.g. of Egypt, China, Poland—Cuba? Contrasts between desert and irrigation, talk about Stalin, Mao, God and reverse, 'Tell me what you really think about us?' Russian Imperialism, about Indian Newspapers, crime in USSR—not reported do not read'. President, Chairman,

Sultan: same, new Czars, 'What will you do when you become PM'?' 'I am a small man, things will change, call me as Ambassador, bad times coming'—The sleeping Uzbek, 90% do not think, Freedom v/s Bread or Freedom and Bread, visit mosque in Kokand, the graves, the public law, displays, European painting section, school children, fountains, canal, entertained by only Maulvi, fruits, peasant with water melon, translated, flowers, some leading questions e.g. land, students, stoppage of religion, its revival, the new...pair, the drive back.

India Pak, religion etc.
'Have not elaborated on'
'No perfect state ever or system' EU
'How do you get a job?' JS
Eu's views on Stalin
—European lavatory habits EU + incidentally Russian too
rolls made from ......
Mullah's pride (in Egitaly's English)
EU's Uzbeknen.

The thalamic roots of Islam go back many centuries. This great thought was itself not ignorant of Christianity, or Judaism and the myths and rites of Christianity have an ancestry that goes back through India, Sumeria, Babylon, to the Neolithic man, to magic, to animism. So what the Commissar was then boarding up was not just mosques, but the very psyche of a vast segment of its own people, who though now subject, are spread like a giant scimitar on the Southern borders of their (Russian) Empire; from Azerbaijan, the south Caucasus, the Turkmen and Kazhak, and Tajikistan, Uzbekistan to Khirgizia. That Kremlin should itself now rescind all these diktats and once again begin to open up the mosques, undertaking an ambitious programme of renovating them, also 'abandoned madarasas', old forts (symbols of a great a Islamic inheritance or was it a horrible 'feudal' past?), is in itself an admission of great failure by this 'dialectical God'.[41] Its attempts at replacing that 'faith' which waters the thalamic roots of Islam can obviously not succeed.

This whole business of Europeanisation was made synonymous with industrialisation, which alone in turn, was equated to progress. This confusion had started even under Czarist Russia. The impulse of communism was far more determined, thus all these 'developments' came about: roads, buses, cars, schools, hospitals, irrigation etc. But all of them remained a transplant. All these are doubtless totally welcome and certainly the more wholesome aspect of 'totalitarian development'. But in their wake, have also come such alien creatures as 'Russian Rock' and monstrous housing blocks and shortages and queues and this cruel erosion of the social cement of family life. It is difficult to see where all this will lead. Religion, in this irreligious system of governance is not at all dead. It remains just under the surface, longingly, hopefully, in atavistic resignation and with faith nurturing an 'Asian patience' of immeasurable depth, for that occasion and that day to come yet, when these new Czars of Moscow would, inevitably in time, enfeeble. Then? and then the azaan will summon the faithful again, I am sure.

It is quite remarkable that in the USSR, over ninety 'nationalities' should be welded together in the apparatus of a state. But that kind of 'statehood', and the problems of ethnic assertion are not mutually compatible. With each new succession and with each new round of denigrating the previous 'God', progressively the inviolability and sanctity of this seat in Kremlin, its aura of authority shall get eroded. Then the currently quiescent queues for meat and food, now

---

41. The USSR as a federation consisted of states with diverse religions, racial background and culture. To unify this diversity, it sought to template similarity by adoption of "communism' and its imposition as the faith to replace the existing beliefs. This 'dialectical God' spoke of replacing the old faith with the new one without the realisation that human beings believed in structures and value systems linked to a 'past'. This 'obliteration' of the past was easier 'attempted' than done.

submitting meekly to bureaucratic arbitrariness will fall back on those more reliable inner certainties, and then might emerge an 'anti materialistic nostalgia', allergic to this false nationalism and rebelling then against the arrogance of state, and in a curiously inverted manner, not entirely contradictory of the dialectical interpretation of History, the pendulum will then tend to swing back to a mystic, irrational, ethical romanticism, or to the more familiar certainties of Islam.

That famous phrase—'Great Game', which later became both a policy frame and a pursuit was originally Arthur Conolly's. He was a very strange 'colonial ruler', always full of 'faith and love and boundless charity, striving without ceasing for the glory of God and for the good of his fellow men'.[42] He returned from home leave to India through Turkey, Persia and Afghanistan, 'a journey which included being captured by Turcoman slavers during a dash towards Khiva—(where) he was luckily turned loose again—and a journey which fixed in his mind the ambition to visit Kokand and Bukhara'. Do listen to him, on a march with a 'Persian caravan', and he was only twenty-two then: 'We felt the air bracing rather than unpleasantly cold, and.... we rode socially along in the bright moonlight, chatting with each other or joking aloud, whilst occasionally one of the party would shout out a wild Pushtoo song.... we generally took the first watch and cooked a kettleful which we drank sociably whilst the others were sleeping round us.'[43] And thinking of 'creating a federation of Turkestan's rulers' he wrote to Rawlinson: 'You have a great game, a noble game, before you... we may keep the Russians out of Toorkistan altogether, if the British Government would only play the grand game'. And thus was born the 'Great Game'.

Predictably, and I was not averse to doing so, on the road to Kokand, Egitaly engaged me in a lengthy conversation. This road carries a fairly heavy load of traffic, cars, buses, lorries, scooters, also

---

42. *Journey to Khiva;* p.155; by Phillip Glazebrook; pub. Kodansha International.
43. ibid.

tractors from adjacent communes. It was therefore, dotted with traffic-police posts. At one of these there was a little farm. I asked Egitaly:

'Why a private farm for traffic-police post?'

'Oh! So they can rest, sit in the shade, eat grapes.' A casual, jovial, deceptive reply.

'Is there a speed limit?'

'Yes, on paper, forty, in real not. When traffic post near all obey rules. Afterwards only two per cent do.'

That was an endearing admission. Horns are freely used, with a kind of herdsman's abandon. Traffic, though, is amongst the more disciplined of any Asian town barring Singapore. One side of the road is barren, on the other where irrigation has reached, lie lush green crops in this fertile valley of Ferghana—poplars, reminiscent of Kashmir, and orchards, and fields with ripe corn and vegetables, for it is high summer. On both sides of the road lie collective farms, women carrying head loads of grass cut for 'private cows', otherwise working languidly in this mid-day heat as any sensible labour would in someone else's field. Villages, with fodder stored on roofs, and mud walls, and children (happy, healthy) playing in the alleys. At the corner of a private house, an enterprising Uzbek has installed an air pump and tends to the flattened tubes of passing motorists. I halt and peep shamelessly into a 'private home': a courtyard near which, UE informs me, is the 'Mehman Khana',[44] 'You know women do not come in front of visitors.' Inside, some grapevines, a patch of corn, a hencoop, and a cattleshed with tethered cows. Every inch of space put so caringly to use; this indomitable assertion of human individuality.

We halt at an Uzbek 'Chaikhana'. Old men sitting on the 'takth'— wooden seat, in the cool shade of a Chinar, nearby a flowing canal; ceremonious and elaborate greetings, deference to elders. A 'dumba', (ram) tethered nearby, its tail obscenely fat. UE is very keen for me

---

44. 'Mehman Khana'—a word which means 'Guest Room'.

to eat 'samosa', (Yes, but it is called 'samos'. Where did it originate?).
I am, as usual, my abstemious self when it comes to eating. Tea arrives.
Successive cups are drunk and every time that which is left is casually
flicked over into the nearby canal. An inquisitive neighbour enquires
something of Egitaly. Laughingly he turns to me and says, 'You know,
Mr. Singh, what he asks? He says are there any rich in India?'

So I say, 'yes'. He says, 'Why don't they do away with them?'

I answer because 'then all will be poor', and he goes into a
prolonged, really heartfelt laugh.

Egitaly breaks a twig of tulsi (basil) growing nearby and hides it
behind his back as if to surprise me. I ruin his pleasure by a totally
needless boast: 'Oh, I know what that is. We have that in India, too.'
For minutes after that I am silenced by an acute consciousness of
my own, though unpremeditated, yet thoughtless insensitivity to
the obvious delights of my kind host. UE is as open hearted in his
hospitality as are most other inhabitants of the desert. It is all so
staggeringly familiar. A sincere and open generosity of spirit, which
will not hesitate to empty out an already impoverished purse, and
all for the convenience and benefit of a guest. For all the time that
UE has been with me, he has not let me pay for a single thing, not
a single time.

'Tell me, Mr. Singh,' we are on the road again, 'how elections held
in your country? Is their cheating and money and people stuffing
paper into....' Here he makes motions of hurried, clandestine,
stamping and stuffing paper into boxes.

I explain as honestly and as best as I can, admitting to many
imperfections. 'And what about your elections, Egitaly?'

'Oh! With us people elected before elections!,' and he joins me
in laughing delightedly at his own joke and at the ridiculousness of
the system. Then more soberly: 'But you know, Soviet Constitution,
best in the world,' I do not immediately dispute it for he is continuing,
'but only if we do what it say, otherwise piece of paper.'

How am I to explain to him how near he is to the bone and how
we all face problems that are not at all dissimilar?

'But you have 99.9% people voting in most elections and all seem to be voting for one party.' I go back to elections and their methodology here.

'Yes, no sick, no dead, no ill, they take boxes to hospitals, railways and,' here he looks at me chuckling, 'we have no opposition,' and he dusts his hands, as if disposing off an unpleasant problem, an inconvenient presence, a bad smell and breaks into loud laughter again.

'Egitaly, did you choose to work for Intourist?'

'No, I was teacher. They, they, (who are these 'they'? Ubiquitous, all powerful?), said you work for Intourist. So here.'

'And for fourteen years you have done this job?'

'Yes.'

'And after fourteen years you get hundred and fifty roubles?' I query. He is too pained to answer. He looks at me, shrugs, and looks out of the car window.

'Tell me, Egitaly, who get the best pay.'

'The army. Every three years they add a star and more money.'

'Why did you not join the army?'

'Too much...' and at a loss for words here, he makes the mock gesture of a salute. But he is a true nationalist if he is anything, so he repeatedly demonstrates that and now also.

'But Russian army best in the world. How you say most...' unhelpfully, I wait, for I want him to persist with his efforts. 'If they say seven o'clock, then one minute this way...' he points threateningly at his watch dial and simultaneously makes a clicking sound in his throat and a gesture of slitting it.

'Disciplined,' I interject, rather unimaginatively at this stage.

'Yes, disciplined. Best discipline in the world. All the time....'

He goes into a demonstration of discipline by sitting up from his slouched position in the car and making gestures of repeated salutes in all directions.

'Then what are you doing in Afghanistan?' I more 'shoot' the question then ask, hoping to catch him unwary.

'We are there to help the people of Afghanistan,' instantly comes this tutored, unconvincing reply, followed immediately thereafter by loud laughter; Egitaly laughing at himself for giving such a reply; at me for asking such an unintelligent and patently obvious question; and at this whole system which generates such falsehoods. Obviously, Afghanistan weighs heavily on his mind, for worriedly he then asks me, both of us having lapsed into silence in the meantime.

'Tell me about Afghanistan,' I do my honest, as unbiased best as I possibly can, for repeatedly he has been emphasising: 'We are talking like friends with open hearts.'

'Even the poor people of Afghanistan, is what we do, not good for them?' He is really seeking reassurance, a bit hopelessly but nevertheless clutching. Sadly, I am unable to do even that.

'And what do people think of Babrak Karmal?' UE.

'Babrak Karmal? Who is Babrak Karmal?' It is for a moment only that he fails to catch the irony and begins an explanation; then stopping and looking at me he breaks into a loud guffaw.

'You know, Egitaly,' I am pressing home my advantage now, 'communism says that the state belongs to workers and peasants.'

'Yes.'

'Then what is happening in Poland now?'

'Yes, wrong, all wrong,' he is distressed, genuinely so but also angry.

'And Poland says they send coal, meat to USSR,' I add provokingly. UE is furious now, contemptuous, angry, 'All these small countries they say friend with Soviet Union, then take, take, take….,' frantic, collecting gestures with both hands and then continuing in the same vein, 'after they have what they want, USSR good bye. Look at China, Egypt, now Poland, not yet but may be tomorrow, Cuba.' Continuing, 'If USSR not send all things it do, we can all live like Brezhnev, we so rich.'

I am astonished at the violence of his reaction. Is it his Uzbek sense of provocation in the face of ingratitude or is it the result of some collective indoctrination, I wonder?

We get to talking about Kokand. The subject of Poland was proving to be explosive (forerunner of things to come?). I ask if it was formerly ruled by a Khan, Emir, Sultan or what?

'What difference does it make, Mr. Singh—Khan, Sultan, President, all mean same thing.' That I could hardly dispute, for that without doubt is ancient Asian wisdom speaking.

'There has never been a perfect state, never will be.' This is not fatalism; this is reality, I think to myself but query, 'And what about Stalin?'

'You know, Mr. Singh, when Stalin die I was in school and I cry, for all books, all books,' he repeats emphatically, 'say he Father of Nation and in his time plenty of things. You get what you want. We have no money then, but if you have you can buy. Now more money, less things.'

Upon reaching Kokand, UE drives straight to a mosque. It is next to the bazaar, an old mosque currently being renovated. We enter a cool, spacious courtyard. Shady trees and grapevines and that musty, timeless atmosphere of all neglected places of worship. Respectfully UE points out the maulvis. One, an old Uzbek of exquisite frailty and a sparse, snow-white beard, sitting composed silent and dignified in an aloof, relaxed manner. He is the senior mullah, UE informs me. A jacketed, more modern version with a neatly trimmed beard, small, cautious, beady eyes and an unctuous manner comes forward and with elaborate courtesy welcomes me. We launch into mutual praise and expressions of simulated delight, and assurances of everlasting friendship between Hindustan and Uzbekistan. I get somewhat carried away by my thesis of tracing roots of history and searching for Babur and common links and all such other sentiments, not at all insincere though, in what I say. Neither is the mullah. UE is, of course, delighted to play this important role of an interpreter, as if his translations had acquired international significance. We take a walk then through the cemetery—well tended and looked after. The portion where the Emir and his families were buried is wisely kept locked. It is behind high walls and an elaborate gate. Some workmen half-heartedly do the job of one. It is hot. UE is exhausted, having kept up late, drinking, ('between us twelve we finished eight bottles of Vodka' he had earlier volunteered—I am staggered by such prodigious capacity), and my sympathies are truly with him. To do this 'back breakingly' boring task of a guide in this still heat and with a late night behind him, I tell him so. He waves my concerns away but does not fail to add 'Let us go and eat the mullah's melons!'

A feast of fruits has been laid out by the mullah. More speeches and more interpretation. Then an invocation to 'Khuda', in which I willingly, but rather unpracticedly join. Follow more of elaborate offers of 'eat this, eat that'. UE advises me to start with the bread. While we are thus eating and whiling away the afternoon heat, a peasant arrives with a watermelon and deferentially offers it to the mullah, who with an ecclesiastical sense of his rights, in a manner that befits a true feudal, also the proper form—accepts it with the most perfunctory of greetings and with no expressions of gratitude at all, as if it were his right to receive, and the duty of the peasant to give. I am warmed to the core of my heart at this demonstration of continuity. The mullah is flowery and profusely vocal, keeping poor UE from eating. My pointed questions about 'How much land under the mosques? How many students in the madarsa etc?' are not only parried with practiced ease, the mullah manages to interject panegyrics about the Soviet system as well. He deserves, every inch, to be the mullah of this distant out-post of Islam, a tiny drop of an Island of Islam in this atheistic sea of heresy. Just as the elaborate farewells have been concluded arrives a pair to get married. 'For nikah?' I enquire, 'Yes', 'Nikah'; 'Nikah' are the delighted replies. They want to be photographed. Outside the courtyard is another pair waiting their turn. 'The mullah is not the only one busy today, married people also very busy later,' adds UE with earthy realism and freedom from false prudery.

A cursory round of the Emir's old palace and we are on our way.

'Tell me, Mr. Singh, what you do, what first thing when you become president?' We have barely got out of the limits of Kokand, where when I wanted to photograph a donkey-cart UE had neatly dissuaded me by saying, 'Why you want to photograph donkey, plenty of donkeys in India!' I wish I could admit that I too had laughed honestly and uproariously then.

But his earlier question coming when it did, as it did, was both flattering and bewildering. I was perplexed, 'Why do you ask that?'

'You think so much about such things, someday you will become something, my mind say. I hope PM, president or such thing.'

There is no appropriate reply to such questions, perhaps, never can be, and my attempt was patently unsatisfactory to UE. No doubt on account of my failure to answer him properly, on account of his hangover, and the mullah's feast, he nodded off to sleep in the by now well above hundred kilometers per hour speeding car. A traffic post near Ferghana slowed us down and also woke him up. He yawned, rubbed his eyes, smacked his dry lips and mouth and then suddenly: 'Are there any limit on how much wealth in India?' In this mid-day heat of the Central Asian Valley of Ferghana I attempt to explain to UE, as best as I can, the finer refinements of the Indian tax laws. It was a futile effort any way, so provocatively, hoping to wake him up.

'But there are many rich people in USSR also, Egitaly.'

'Where?' looking around in mock search. There is a smile on his face, and in his eyes. He may have only just woken up but he is already alert, this UE.

'Look at all your new Czars?'

'Where?' he persists obdurately, but smilingly, 'where?'

I reply, 'All the new Czars are in India,' and we both laugh at these mad, mad systems.

Under the Chinar lined streets of Ferghana, UE takes hold of my hand, 'When you become PM or president, remember me, call me to India as ambassador. Together we will change things!'

It is 2 a.m. again. Even if I wanted to, I could not add to what UE said as a conclusion. There is so much of what he said that I have not been able to elaborate. Most of it is there in the notes.

Of course, not all. It is, in any case, impossible to faithfully recreate a living person on paper, or to fully reproduce a conversation.

I had started my trip to Ferghana and Kokand hesitantly, but I am so glad I went. I would have missed a very great deal otherwise.

From Usmanov Egitaly I have learnt more about USSR than from all other symbols of 'progress', though, so much of what he said is left out.

What a memorable visit it has been to Ferghana, Babur's birthplace. UE would no doubt laugh, or perhaps cry, if I told him I have, after all, been able to trace some indefinable links.

Notes
To Machiavelli, on death bed the Cardinal's advise: 'Give up the path of the Devil' even now....'
   Machiavelli, hoarsely, 'This is no time to break relations and make enemies.'
   1914 a Brussilov offensive: front rank: Boots and Rifles
   2nd rank: Boots only
   3rd neither! Pick up from the dead. For 4 years for the Czar, then for Kerensky, then the Bolsheviks, then the Red Army! Incredible.

Notes
Departure from Fergana hectic account, UE's lateness.
   'All this for 150 Rbls,' 'I am busy all time,' when three groups come I go mad, 'Remember our talk'—Embraces and
   kisses me on both cheeks on the tarmac, next to the aircraft, again relieved not lips.
   Austrian student from Innsbuck, tedious question about Democracy/Bureaucracy in Fergana
   Museum: Tashkent the museums: History/Applied arts.
   Poland—'Solidarity wants to finish socialism.'
   'Uzbekistan from feudalism to socialism—jumping capitalism.'
   —Abdul Momeen an Afghanistan (cautiously, carefully) my queries on milk, meat (his salary is 120 Rbls).

A single American School teacher journeying between Praha:
Moscow, Leningrad, Minsk,
Trans Siberian Railway: Irkutsk, Khobrovsk back, Tashkent and
outs:
Prim, catholic and pretty self assured—from Philadelphia—old
American women are formidable, more so, when mid-aged or old.
The smooth Intourist Manager—about 'Alem—Ata'.

Notes
Substance: Questions
Myth and reality; bread and / or freedom; Means-ends;
Communism and Fascism; direct suppression truth; indirect
suppression—denial of facts, twisting of events, direct propagation
of untruth.

Soviet Xenophobia
Propaganda, equation, socialism—industrialization; In USSR
industrial revolution came after the revolution —For Marxism it
was a precondition not a consequence. Political education:
history is neither squeamish nor sentimental; Feudalism—
Capitalism—Socialism (incentives?) 'Collectivism v/s
individualism', 'voluntary discipline v/s legal coercion'; communal
responsibility, international class solidarity, dignity of labour,
replace God, reform v/s retribution, persuasion instead of
compulsion—etc. etc. what mockery—Russian Power politics
and expansionism.
'Nationalised economy always becomes an instrument of
tyranny, corruption and patronage.'

P.S.

As an afterthought I add now—not in my earlier writing of this
travelogue: 'Is it not ironical, also illustrative that one of Gorbachev's
first steps upon assuming power in 1985,' writes Francine du Plessix
Gray in her *Soviet Women,* was to 'purge the Central Committee
of Uzbekistan's Communist Party; as exposed by his regime, the

network of graft and racketeering which had thrived...during the rule of Uzbek Party Chairman Sharif Rashidov—a lethal gangster, worshipped like a mediaeval khan by the Communist Party's local hierarchy—(He) made the Gambino family's scandals look like kindergarten candy sales'.

The Three 'Half' Journeys

Khiva (Uzbek)
Ashkabad (Turkmen)
Almaty (Kazhak)

These three 'half journeys', otherwise memorable, remained 'half'
for they were constrained by time, by circumstance also by events.

They are still incomplete, holding a promise and an assurance,
for I have a mystical conviction about travelling always to these
lands, better then to feel satiated or falsely complete—to shut this
door of travel across the Amu Darya? How can I?

Khiva

ALONG THE LOWER AMU DARYA LIES THAT GREAT OASIS–KHIVA: this remote, ancient outpost of many kingdoms; it was earlier Khwarazm, then later ancient Khorazm, until finally Khiva emerged as a state.

Khiva has always been greatly sought after, but for different reasons in different periods of time, and it has always remained difficult to reach. Deserts surround it on three sides (almost)—the forbidding wastes of Kara-Kum and the Kyzyl-Kum, presenting near impossible obstacles, thus denying access even to the most intrepid and the determined. Water, obviously, has always not just been scare, it has largely not been there at all in the surrounding deserts. That is also why this oasis of Khiva was the destination of so many caravans on the ancient Silk Road. Heat here in summer often crosses fifty degrees during day, plummeting by twenty-five to thirty degrees at night; and the cold during winter is always dry, brittle and arctic in its intensity; the sand storms of the Kara-Kum, blinding. This was the ancient state of Khorezm, today's Khiva, in the north and west of Uzbekistan that I had long dreamt of visiting, even more then Bukhara.

Khwarazm, after all was one of the oldest centres of civilisation in central Asia. It was already a part of the Achaemenid Empire of

Cyrus the Great in the sixth century BC, freeing itself from that hold only some two hundred years later. India, too, had reached here; it is said 'Indians were amongst the early inhabitants, some adhered to Zoroastrianism and used Aramaic script' an assertion that has always intrigued me because the equation just does not seem to work—not historically, but I like the sound of it. It was the Arabs that conquered Khwarazm in the seventh century and it is they that brought Islam here. Around 995 CE a united country emerged, with Urgench as the capital and as a 'major seat of Arabic', just around the time that Mohammed Ghori was first stepping into India. Stability was followed by prosperity and the Khanate reached great heights of power, its rule then spreading from the 'Caspian to Bhukara and to Samarkand'. In 1221, arrived Genghiz and inevitably Khiva was razed to the ground, but he did include it in the 'Golden Horde'. Practically, and in consequence, trade followed conquest, for the caravans that came, brought commerce in the wake of the Mongols, and this at great profit to Khwarazm. Yet again, it rose and flowered, until the arrival of Timur who again destroyed it along with its vast 'irrigation systems'. There then followed 'a century of struggle over Khwarazm between the Timurids, the descendants of Timur, and the 'Golden horde'. 'This was followed by a founding of the Uzbek state... the khanate of Khiva', and of this khanate, Khiva become the capital.

It is odd how fluidly centuries arrive and depart in such narrations, conquests and conquerors and destruction alone finding space—magnificent forts and mosques and madarasas, the rulers, yes, but not much about the ruled. Not to much avail though, for events and personages and empires are all—all always ground to dust by time—and relentlessly. Time remembers nothing, forgets nothing, never stops to reflect or regret, it keeps flowing endlessly.

I had always found the very inaccessibility of Khiva (now, of course, only relatively so) as its great attraction; that was the magnet that drew me unceasingly. And yet it took me many years before I could reach it. But I was not alone in my failures. Czarist Russians, had also tried to reach Khiva, to actually conquer Khiva. But whenever they sought to do so, the protecting deserts always defeated them. Three Russian failures had preceded Peter the Great's efforts through Beckovitch Cherkassky, who had set out in 1717, with ambitious plans for silting 'gold from the sands of the Oxus and turning that river back into its old course so that it might empty into the Caspian'.[45] At first thirst and heat destroyed 'a quarter of the force'. What happened to the remaining thousand is a harrowing tale. They were 'invited into Khiva by the Khan with the suggestion that, so as to be sure of comfortable quarters for all, they should be divided up into seven handy parties', and billeted in 'different parts of the town'. Obviously a massacre had to follow. Thereafter, over a century went by without any repeat of any military effort, not until December 1839, 'when General Peroffski led 5,000 men out of Orenburg to march on Khiva, giving the plight of the Russian captives sold there in the slave market as the excuse. He had chosen the cold season instead of the heat and drought which had been so fatal to Cherkassky'.[46] But he had misjudged gravely for winter in the 'Kyzil Kum is no less severe'. His transport of five thousand camels had nothing to feed on.... 'They died in hundreds, the men in turn froze. Peroffski sent his czar a message, which needs recounting: 'Obstacles which no foresight can take account of run counter to the success of the expedition'.

Khiva was, amongst other trading items and other goods (for it was always a renowned trading post), the centre of the slave trade in the region. But here in the heart of Central Asia, it were the 'Russian and Ciracassion white slaves' that were the most sought after. It is by this improbable thread that hangs a very moving and a near impossible account of Captain Shakespeare, all of twenty-eight years old, bringing out 418 of these Russian slaves and then safely marching them to Orenburg. But to that we revert later.

---

45. *Journey to Khiva* by Phillip Glazebrook; p.180; pub. Kodansha International.
46. *ibid*; p.181.

Early in my school days, and somewhat precociously too, I had read avidly about it (Abbott and Connolly and Burns and the intrepid Mohan Lal). But the sheer gall of Captain Shakespeare was breathtaking. His extraordinary exploit of marshalling the 418 captive from their owners' hiding places, talking them out, and actually riding dangerously back overnight into Khiva from his first camp to impertinently demand of the Khan that one particularly 'beautiful Russian child', who earlier had been promised to be released but was actually concealed at the time of releasing the Russian slaves must now be released. And he succeeded in achieving that and then 'shepherded his party over eight hundred miles, across this formidable desert until he reached Orenburg and the Sea'.

It was finally General Kaufmann who marched as the conqueror of Khiva in 1873. Physically, though Khiva remained unchanged: 'a wasp's nest' for the intricacy of its streets and courts; and so it travelled in time, essentially 'unaltered since … Alexander the great'.[47] It is that Khiva which Burnaby also describes as having 'hardly changed in the 1920s'. This Khiva lasted until the renovators 'invaded the town in the 1960s' under Soviet tutelage. But more was yet to follow. In mid-nineteenth century a 'great character' appeared: (July 1843) 'that oddest of Anglican clergymen, Dr. Joseph Wolff, who set out to discover if Stoddart and Conolly were still alive, as he 'believed them to be' made his presence known. His departure from England was arresting: In October, Wolf set out from Southampton to 'beard the tyrant at Bokhara', as he proclaimed, leading Captain Grover, a promoter of the Reverend to remark 'any stranger witnessing his departure would have thought he was taking a trip to the Isle of Wight'.[48]

And this redoubtable Reverend Wolf actually reached Khiva, returned to England, and then wrote a quaint but fascinating account of the whole adventure, *Mission to Bukhara*.

---

47. ibid; p.202.
48. *Captain Grover and the Bokhara Victims* p.269.

Mahmud Pahalwan

Finally, I was leaving, early in the morning, bound for Khiva. My last visit to Uzbekistan had actually been and had also felt so totally incomplete without Khiva. All these thoughts now came flooding back: The Khorezm region and the Oasis, Amu Darya, and the desert of Kara-Kum and all that.

The plane, blessedly a charter, was not bound by any schedules. We therefore, left at 8.30 a.m. Even then the Tashkent sun was hot and at that early hour, uncomfortable. A sparse haze obscured the sky, trapping rather then letting the heat escape, and when air borne I saw the same haze spread below, even as we winged North Westwards.

The desert is so near at hand; it appears immediately after we were air-borne and continued endless, entirely treeless. Not a single shadow, not one tree, or bush to relieve the relentlessness of the land, not one living thing moving or visible from that height.

It is at Urgench that we land; the city that the invading Arabs had established. Unlike the last time it was with ceremony that I was received now, but this made me sorely miss the freedom and privacy of the back-packer that I was then. Until of course, Khorzem, where Uzbek girls in their best finery received me with flowers. A car drove me to Khiva, just about thirty kilometers away.

The many tiers in full view

What had been dreamt of for years, has atleast happened, though, not as I wanted. I am finally in Khiva: The place, the people, the attitudes, the architecture, the ambience where am I? I wonder, is it Barmer? Or Jaisalmer? This is so like home. But in a totally different setting, a different time. These city environs of Khiva, these mud caked walls, all these could easily be the desert outposts of Shahgarh, or Kishengarh, or even Jaisalmer. The sky so blue, so absolutely cloudless and so completely matching in its openness, the wide open spaces of the desert,… is this why I have so longed to be here? Songs and dances and feasts and festivities have been laid out for me, though with the intricacies of water borne plumbing there remains still the same reassuring unfamiliarity, as we have in our environs.

The monuments of Khiva attracted me greatly. It was the pavilion of Mahmud Pahalwan that I was seeking, by myself, to savour and to imbibe the flavour of, but alone I could not be. The guide inflicted upon us, as all guides do—(displaying proudly his gold capped teeth and a chest card announcing that he was a 'Director')—unbearable statistical details of building and personages of old. How India countinues to live here—from memory till today. Mahmud Pahalwan and the myth of Rai and his daughter's 'swayamwar in India',[49] incredible that this is the phrase used by the guide; he shows me a pillar with one particular floral pattern, being emphasised, especially to me by the guide, who, of course, totally unembarrassedly but almost proudly acknowledging, 'that this is Shiva!' This depiction and this too, in a mosque in Khiva, showing 'Shiva and his symbols'! It felt as if some root had been traced by coming to Khiva.

It was getting uncomfortably hot by the time I left for Ashkabad in Turkmenistan.

---

49. 'Swayamwar'—A ceremony where a bride could select her husband from the assembled princes. She had the right to garland any prince and she became his queen. This was an ancient Hindu custom.

Ashkabad

I CANNOT ACCOUNT FOR THE LIGHTNESS OF THE AIR IN ASHKABAD. It feels so much fresher, and markedly less grim than in Khiva or Tashkent. And Turkmen women (not so the men) are slimmer and not at all mongolid in features; they are doe-eyed and ravishingly beautiful. In the South lies the low, furrowed range of Kopetdag Mountains beyond which spreads Persia—Iran; to the North are the deserts and the Aral Sea, as indeed are the deserts to the East. In a westerly direction, at not too great a distance is the Caspian. Perhaps it is this combination of sea, mountain and desert that counts for the air here.

It was a very short visit that I could make, not satisfactory at all in that sense. The options were limited, of the yes 'or' no variety—either accept this one day opportunity, or none at all. Obviously, I chose the former. If not any other gain I would certainly be able to achieve my lifelong ambition of seeing the great Akhal-Teke breed of horses in their natural environs, for it is special to Turkmenistan. I had been drawn to this breed by the knowledge that Alexander's great war horse, Bucaphelus, astride which he had reached the gates of India, was of the Akhal-Teke breed. Bucaphelus died on the edge

A troop of Akhal-Teke on a night march

Author at a Stud farm

of India, villages both in India and in Pakistan exist now named after this horse.

'The Akhal–Teke is an exotically beautiful, extravagantly graceful and versatile breed of riding horse. It is highly regarded for its speed, stamina, comfortable gaits, intelligence and trainability. It is also arguably the oldest surviving cultured equine breed. Its extraordinary physical power and sensitive nature is derived from the highly specialized conditions requiring "partnership" with the nomad tribes of Central Asia.'[50]

The breed's name dates to the end of the nineteenth century, comprising two words: 'Akhal,' the long oasis nestled in the foothills of the Kopet Dag, and 'Teke,' after the Turkmen tribe, the dominant nomadic people who inhabited this oasis, even as centuries of volatile waves of human movement, throughout much of Central Asian history, bypassed this isolated Akhal oasis.

---

50. www.imh.org/imh/bw/akhal.html.

Almaty

With the Kazakhs

Fine warriors the Kazakhs, they lived here by farming and cattle-breeding and steered their combat chariots with ease and expertise; of which, there can still be seen images drawn on rocks, the locations where these 'ancients had arranged their temples and sanctuaries with only the firmament as their cover'. On cliffs burnt black by the sun still exist chiselled 'scene of dances'; image of Sun as deity and camels and bulls as ancient Gods. This is also where lie burial mounds of noble warriors, though scattered all through the Kazakh steppes: magnificent mounds and burial vaults, like the necropolis in the steppers of Sary-Arka and Tagiskent in the Transaral area. These 'fine warriors, shepherd and farmers' had also perfected metallurgy. And with pride, I was informed that it is here that was initiated 'development of copper', practiced to this day in the Zhezkazgan and Sayak copper quarries. The Sakas arrived here, 'Saks' for the ancient Persians, 'se' for the Kazakhs, for the Greek's Scythians. Because they were essentially nomadic they were natural horseman, too. In fact the Sakas were the first 'ever horsemen in the world to master the use of the bow and arrow at full gallop'. Was it before the invention of the stirrup, I keep wondering.

In the fifth and sixth centuries BC, 'Saks', so inform various scholars, established their centre in south-east Kazakhstan. Their kings were also simultaneously their priests, they had a written language and mythology of their own and were known for their well developed art.[51]

I read again through my diary notes on this travel in Kazakhstan and found a rather uncertain sounding note. When recording thus, as above, or as on previous pages and diaries, an impression of always being in exotic places, this perpetual romance and glamour of travel inevitably gets created. That, alas is not so at all. Of course, there is this continuing thrill of travel, of reaching the new, the unseen... but not always. Often sheer weariness overtakes and as I recorded then: 'my present physical and mental state prevents me from doing so much of what I want to; such wrenching fatigue accompanies me these days'.

And yet I travel, constantly. I reflect, too, constantly on—'My Journey'—from where I had started and where I am now. Also, when travelling thus, I have always most wanted a certain freedom to make choice, even routine choices like when to halt, where to go, when to stand still and to savour... to just stand, to have that needed space and also record impressions of the immediate before they fade from memory and consciousness, but too many others clamour for that space.

It is early here in Almaty, 6:30 a.m.—and still dark and silent outside. I reached here in the afternoon yesterday. It was Sunday; the feel was of a city at ease. The stamp of communism, of Soviet Union still very much there, all over: the grand central plaza and the imposing but sadly ugly 'House of People', or similar such euphemisms; besides, which self respecting president of Central Asian Republic would now not want to have a marble palace?

---

51. From www.kazakhastan.orexca.com/kazakhastan_history.shtml.

Almaty sits at the very end, the tail as it were of the beauteous Tien Shan, and for me they (Tien Shan) are amongst the most beautiful of mountain ranges. Snow clad or bare, craggily they ring Almaty on one side, like giant walls of a super human citadel.

I wanted to move out, to leave the city, to be in the Kazakh steppes, to savour the freedom of this enormous space, to breathe that air, also to escape this entrapment of officialdom. I did finally leave Almaty but officialdom did not leave me. Because I wanted to be left alone, and to go into the country, to any horse fair in any village, I was escorted to a 'selected one'.

When we reached, the snuffling village dogs went into an orgy of hysterical barking, and then before I had even realised what was happening they were kicked aside by my anxious hosts, yelping and protesting and crying. Poor dogs, they were doing what any dog would. But my hosts, anxious to create a 'good impression', wanted no village dog's interfering in their proceedings. I tried to put them at ease, for they were kind and were doing everything possible to make me feel at home. Precisely because we were trying so hard for some time, neither of us succeeded in achieving our respective objectives, or for that matter achieving anything. The village headman then took over. A swarthy, gypsy-esque figure, tall, with a manner that denoted natural ease with office, also with ordering others. 'We will see a horse race,' he announced, then 'Let us go'. So we walked up a hillock and there below, milling was an untidy troop of horses, with riders of a great spread of age groups from pre-adolescent children to almost post middle-age seniors. They were all preparing to participate in this 'horse race'—no order, no procedure, just a melee of enthusiastic Kazakhs. 'How will you judge? And do all start at the same time?' I had asked.

'Oh! That is not important. They have to race for about fifteen kilometers, all get sorted out.'

'Fifteen kilometers. Where? In a course?'

'Course? The steppe is there, that is an endless course. Besides, it is only fifteen kilometers to gallop.'

And then they were all off, going round our hillock, to some distant clump of trees and then back-around the hillock and back again. The pace was competitive, fast—the whip—not at all for show; it was for using and was being used with abandon, almost ceaselessly, mercilessly. The horses, of some variety in colour, conformation and age, remaining quite immune to all this.

Suddenly, somebody fell, I could see he was very young, a boy really, his galloping mount had also by then halted and begun to graze unperturbed, almost immediately and not much troubled. There was no concern, no anxiety, barely any comment amongst the spectators. I was worried, the boy lay motionless; then suddenly his legs, then the rest of his body began twitching uncontrollably, while he was still unconscious. By now I was really alarmed and gave voice to that. The village headman remained nonchalant: 'He is all right, shortly he will mount and race again.' And sure enough he did do that, after about ten minutes or so. The 'race' meanwhile had continued all the time, without any interruptions.

From this 'race' I was escorted to a feast, a 'Kazakh Yurt Lunch', again somewhat of a 'put-up' show, for the feast had already all been

A Khazahak Yurt

The delicate moves of a Khazak girl

spread out, on the outskirts of the village, near a cool stream and in the shade of giant trees. 'Kumis' flowed freely, so thereafter did tongues. Gifts were then exchanged and a full set of robes and a tall Kazakh hat was mine, no, not simply to see, to actually wear. Great merriment followed at this combination of my attire. The warmth of late spring, the vicinity of a flowing stream, plentiful Kumis feast and merriment inevitably led to: 'Mr Singh, you now like a Khan we should get you married again' offered othe headman. Loud guffaws in the gathering, endorsed the suggestion. 'I am old for that. Can't you see' rather lamely responded, both embarrassed and confused. 'No-no-no-you tell him what a man can do';—the headman—my host to my young female guide and interpreter: 'Men? Men never grow old. My uncle is almost eighty, he married again and a son has come.' She saucily informed me and yet again the cry of 'marriage' went up from a host of kumis drenched voices.

Early the next day we left Almaty, the aircraft circling a few times in the bowl of this capital to gain height and then headed directly south, for India. In this small craft we were to wing our way over countries that were magical even in their names: Kazakhstan, Uzbekistan, Tadjikistan, Afghanistan then Pakistan and finally India. And we were to fly over the great mountain chains of Central Asia, too.

This became truly a most memorable journey. To my great good fortune it was a day of unmatched clarity and also early enough so that neither cloud nor haze obscured our view. We flew over these

Tien Shan

great convulsions of mountain ranges, the Hindu Kush, the Tien Shan and the Pamir Knot; there they lay below—snow clad, craggy, knife edged ridges, with great white meadows of ice and snow pouring through funnel shaped valleys; glaciated, creased and crevassed wherever the descent was steep and where forced to steeper accelerated descent, it broke into knife edged serrations— mile upon mile upon mile.

This great turmoil of mountains continued as far as the vision could go—to the east to Chitral, Skardu, Ladakh, the plateau of Tibet and the great Himalayan range. A momentous, breathtaking view, memorable, and to the west—the desert; in the south the rugged, barren ranges around Afghanistan—beyond which lay India.

Frunze

With the Khirgiz

Notes from my Diary

- Hotel Ala—Too (Snow Capped Mountains)
- Monument to fighters: Amazon called Urkia: Khirgiz 1st Chief of Collective Farm
- Ok To Gul (Poet)—'No Khirgiz script' until 1918!
1936—Cyrillic script
- Bazaar
- Monument to 45 heroes—Young league of Comsomol, best pupils as sentries (to inculcate patriotism)—a chance to stand guard for 15 minutes in a year
- Park Oak (Fetisov)
- Theatre of opera and ballet: Maldy backward.....
- Park laid by Fetisov in 1896
(Liberation from Germans)
- Labour Glory
(White House): Central Committee of CPK and Council of Ministers.

History
- Housing Colony, 1825
- Frunze—'Pish Peck'—(Fortress of Kokand Khanate) in a river/ caravan routes leading to inner Tien Shan
3 rivers: Alamedin—Ala Archa—Chu On the conjunction the town.
- Populations:

Khirghizia   :   3.5 million
Frunze   :   1.5 million

- Part of Russian Empire- 1863
- First European influence:
1866: Physical arrival of Russians
1878: The town of Pish Peck is established from a Mily garrison.
1926: Frunze (Gen Mikait Vasilivich Frunze)
Born 1865—Died 1925—(40 yrs)

Conversations with Sajida

'Are you a Communist?' 'No my soul is Communist.'
'I believe what ever the party does is right?' 'Whatever' 'Yes'
'Do you think anything good was done before the Revolution?'
'No.'
'Do you think life started with the revolution?' 'Yes.'
'Khirgizia was a colony of Czarist Russia' 'Yes.'
'Are you not now?'
'We are voluntarily a part of the Union'
'Was there a referendum for that'
'What is referendum?'
'Why are you in Afghanistan?'
'Because of USA and Pakistan attacked it and we have a treaty of friendship with them.'

'You attacked—'

'No' (almost angry now)

'Yes, your State is based on a lie—'

'No, No', (really angry now)

(I am deliberately but unforgivably provocative)

'If India not careful we will do same to India!'

Later: 'Why do you ask about Afghanistan, why not about poor people' and suddenly 'if USA can do counter—revolution, we can do revolution.' The usual mish mash about 'elections in capitalist societies' and in socialist ones?

Money in one, '99.9%' support in another—Deviations from these adopted/accepted (mentally) stabilising points in life lead to an immediate manifestation of hysterical disagreements; then if you persist, to a silent and secret smile as if privy to some inner secret, 'party knows best'; circumlocution, non typical examples; answering by counter questions and finally to the ultimate condemnation—'You are brain washed by Americans.'

8 August: Frunze (now Bishkek)

There was again no one at the Aeroflot desk in Tashkent when I went to check in for my onward flight to Frunze. I waited. There was nothing else to be done in any case. Several unexplainable gaps exist in the 'system'—anxious, black holes of staggering inefficiency. The citizen, when confronted by them is helpless. By and by, however:

'Hello Mr. Singh, welcome, I am Alexander.'

'Hello, Alexander.'

'Do you have ticket?'

'Well, that is necessary is it not for travelling by air?' I am, in hindsight, appalled at my own rudeness, but persist for I was seized by perversity. Alexander was instantly alert. It is so depressing to find that in feudal, fascist, authoritarian, totalitarian societies, rudeness always carries with it the stamp of instant authority. He vanished to return with the woman actually responsible for checking passengers in. Somewhat mollified by now, but only just, I asked Alexander, 'Was Aeroflot on strike all this time?' This conversation did take place, though even its recounting continues to shame me.

'Sorry Mr. Singh, not strike, on dinner!' was the wonderful riposte. I could really not, after that, carry on much further in that vein; as a signal of reconciliation, therefore: 'Where are you from, Alexander?' He became immediately, so much lighter.

'From Armenia.'

'Alexandrovitch Macedonic,' this came from the girl at the counter.

This shamed me even more. India has related to Armenia for so long—our great pilgrimages to Baku. And then through medieval India so much trade existed between us. Alexander beamed and added: 'No, not Alexander the Great, Alexander the Small!' continuing, 'you know, Mr. Singh, girls all over the same—no difference, no difference.'

I am the only Indian 'tourist' going to Frunze. While others go packed like sardines, I have a whole bus to myself! I do not know what but some instinct prompts me to enquire from my escort: 'Where are my bags?' She does not speak English but understands the ward 'baggage', therefore making some reassuring sounds in Russian she motions me to board. I refuse to. The departure area for Intourists, despite all that elaborateness is the same as the service area of the airport. I could therefore see loaders idly loafing about and luggage vans parked haphazardly—these are the bowels of the airport building. I point to the dark recesses, where I know my baggage must find its way from the counters.

The girl asks someone, who asks another and yet another and so it goes on, and could easily have endlessly, until eventually, from the inner recesses of this hall, emerge my two bags. I am triumphant—my intuition had stood by me.

I am on board. Next to me is placed a woman, poor thing, of some uncomfortable proportions, she over-flows her seat and fans herself constantly. I am squashed by the window. In this mid-day heat, the parked aircraft is like the insides of a sauna. The crew is of course indifferent to all this. Soon after we take off my co-passenger starts being sick, and there is only one bag between the two of us, naturally, she must have it. Besides, Frunze is still atleast an hour away.

Now, I do not cite any extenuating circumstance for what followed in Frunze, but the fact does remain that it was a very trying journey. It had been an exasperating check-in, now this, on top of that the heat and finally, to cap it all, the flight, covering as it does the Central Asian steppes in the middle of the day was exceptionally turbulent.

At Frunze there followed another mix-up, there was no Intourist reception. At first I was only amused. It could after all be a repeat of Ferghana and I might end up by finding a Kirghiz equivalent of Egitaly. There was also relief at being finally out of that aircraft. I waited unconcernedly at first, then with a feeling of being cheated and finally in anger.

The new airport of Frunze is a modernistic building: large and impersonal, not like Ferghana. No one pays any attention, and why should they? The signboards, all in Russian are difficult for me—having given up studying this language so long back. I began to fume inwardly. It is to the hotel, that I want to reach, to wash, change, lie back and collect mentally. I enquire of a few. No results. I am misdirected. At that time I had thought otherwise but I do now, in calmer retrospect think that, that was not intentional. The Intourist office lies at the extreme end of this building. A concerned and kindly airport official, suffering dreadfully from indigestion, ('his flatulence, withered flowers', Gabriel Garcia Marquez has written) eventually took me to that office. Inside it was a comfortable but the usual waiting lounge. It had two idle occupants, a man and a middle aged woman, reclining, in this midday heat, taking their ease and watching T.V. I blew my top when the woman, who got up in a hurry, straightening her dress said 'Mr. Singh? Welcome.'

It was a shaming demonstration of ill temper and that, too, at a woman. Inexcusable. No amount of extenuating circumstance, stress, lack of sleep etc. etc. will suffice to erase my shame at the memory of it.

Later, much later, for it is a long drive from the airport, when a woman, named Sajida, my guide and interpreter, informed me that I am the 'first Indian tourist ever to visit Frunze and Khirgizia', I am even more ashamed. When I apologise for my bad behaviour she says: 'I did not think Indians behave like this. They peace loving people. You like Americans. But possibly, you government; not like us ordinary people.'

What does one say to all this? What could I have?

Hotel Ala-Too (Snow capped Mountain) is the most pleasant hotel that I have stayed in so far in the USSR. Wooden planks on the floor are reasonably well polished. A simple Kirghiz carpet lay near the bed and double windows opened out onto an apple orchard. At dinner the waitresses were attentive, but the food sadly as routine as always. Extravagantly, I ventured a glass of white wine. My table stood by a large window, which opened out onto the same orchard. The heat of the day had waned. The sky had slowly darkened; a cool breeze blew in from the distant steppes or is it the mountains? For here the two meet.

In Khirgizia, European Russia arrived quite some time back. It is not alien here. There are chandeliers on the roof, the table linen is finer, and next to me sit couples who could be occupying tables in the Europe of the fifties. There is some pretence at elegance too, but all just that bit shoddy, just that forced. A band, as in all other Intourist hotels, plays the usual 'RR'. Then without warning, an announcement: 'The next song is in honour of our respected guest from friendly India, Mr. Singh!' I am deeply embarrassed by this attention, and manage to raise only a hesitant hand of acknowledgement. The tune is undecipherable. The gesture is touching until I begin to wonder, 'But, who told them? I am no official, I am on my own, I want to remain so.'

The musicians have a rest. The drummer comes and sits next to me and makes conversation in what I presume is English. I try and follow what he is saying, as best as I can.

'A girl wants to meet you, she talks English' he says. I am unwary. 'Yes, with great pleasure. Where is she?'

'She comes soon.' Some warning signals then begin to appear at the back of my mind. 'The drummer', after some desultory effort at talk suddenly gets up and leaves as if in great hurry. Soon thereafter, a girl with a headband and a curious, furtive manner arrives, sits down uninvited and without a bye-your-leave enquires: 'Where are you from?' 'India,' I reply. She gets up and leaves. Now, all this is very curious indeed. I continue with my meal and am just about finishing it when she reappears equally suddenly, sits down as before and more states than asks 'You are from Moscow?' I observe this time that she is drunk. Before I could reply she picks up my wine glass and drains it. 'No, I am from Delhi.' 'I do not believe—you from Moscow.' She is looking around constantly. All this is becoming very embarrassing now. I am worried, somewhat alarmed and beginning to feel quite out of my depth. 'Why do you keep looking around? Is something troubling you?' 'I like Vodka; I want Vodka.' I keep quiet. She is drunk enough. 'There is a policeman here and you are from Moscow.' She repeats the obsession or is perhaps answering my question. I get up to leave. Frantic now she says: 'Fifteen, I come to your room. What room number? Give me fifteen roubles.'

So this is what it is? Not any KGB entrapment, it is really a rather crude pick-up job, prostitution in socialist utopia. I am not delighted at discovering another flaw, if anything a bit saddened. There is a persistent, near violent intensity in all this propositioning. I want to leave without creating a scene. She is drunk enough and could easily cause one. 'Money', its absence, a revolutionary flash—'I am sorry I do not have that much money.' 'Shit,' she exclaims and rushes out.

I take a walk in the park just outside the hotel, more to savour the cool of the evening than anything else. I am not in need of exercise. I eat only once a day in any case and that too frugally because of costs and the quality of food. I am troubled, not by any hypocritically moralistic attitudinising about prostitution, more at the hypocrisy of a system which proclaims its ability to change human nature, on the soulless strength of its materialistic doctrine and admits to no failures. Then why here this breakdown in Khirghizia and not Uzbekistan? The guides in Samarkand and in Bukhara had even declined my offers of cigarettes. The former, in fact, with touching and simple innocence, had told me, 'My father caught me trying a cigarette with a Russian friend. He beat me.' As simple as that. Uncomplicatedly accepting paternal beating as a way of life, a form as old as Asia, as Islam. This has nothing to do with the state. This is private, this manifestation as a characteristic of society. Egitally had asked questions like: 'Mr. Singh, Indian girls all virgin at marriage?' 'Yes,' I had replied, 'a majority of them. Perhaps not so in all cases in the towns but almost invariably in the villages. And what about Uzbekistan?' 'Yes, boys and parents demand all girls virgin.' He had asked on another occasion: 'Mr. Singh, do Indian men and woman, married, go around.' I was a bit slow on catching that. When I did I too, answered truthfully 'Men, yes Egitaly, but by and, large, not women.' He heaved a sigh of relief as if happy, at finding this similarity with us and had said, 'Like with us. We also same.'

This 'pick-up' effort is not such an unusual incident after all, it is noteworthy to me only for where it occurred. It is distressing because, in essence it was gross. Also that in this small, outlying Frunze, a Russian girl, not Kirghiz, adopted this trade and at so much risk. The so-called socialist system is answerable. Its fundamental proposition about the perfection of the 'state apparatus' is to blame for any aberration, too, is it not? Leaders of socialist states never commit errors of judgement; they are 'suprahuman'. In the face of such an impossible assertion a terrible schizophrenia manifests itself whenever unanswerable questions are posed. In the case of the girl if I complain about her or if she is caught, as inevitably and sadly some day she would be, then either the law enforcing authorities will take a frightful 'bribe' from her, or possibly, with total cruelty, despite the 'bribe', she would be put away not for 'prostitution', (that would depict a failure of the state) but for something like 'insanity', or 'betraying the state', or such other cover all. From Evtushenko to Korchonoi and Elya Ehrenberg, to this wayward waif, all can be rounded up under this all-embracing evil of insanity. And such has been the apparent conditioning of the mind of the Soviet citizenry that when faced with such unanswerables, one half of their split personality takes over and accepts the massive lies of the state. e.g. 'Solzhenitsyn is a CIA agent'. They even accused Trotsky, the founder of the Red Army of being that and the schizophrenic personality of the state accepted that too. Or, it perverts truth. It takes a non typical example and blows it up to mean exactly the opposite. Officially, in USSR, there is no prostitution, so if and when this girl is apprehended she would be a 'mental patient'. I had asked Egitaly: 'What about crime in USSR?' 'Crime,' he had answered, 'it not in newspapers, it not recorded, therefore no crime in Soviet Union.' But he had laughed at the absurdity of his own assertions. He had the sturdy commonsense to do so. When, on the other hand, I had asked Abdul Momeen, who incidentally also gets only hundred and twenty roubles, and has to look after a family with a young daughter, about food shortages, he had somewhat hesitantly, but ruefully admitted, 'We are having problem with meat and milk.' 'Why?' 'I am no expert but specialists say our stock-rearing and crop production is suffering because ninety percent of Russia's arable and cultivable lands lie where there is insufficient sunshine and only ten percent with sunshine. But where sunshine, no water, and where no sunshine water': QED. Now this is such an incredible assertion that ordinarily, in the 'imperfect' system of democracies, also carnivorous capitalism it would be greeted with hoots of derisive laughter. Not so in the USSR. Here the 'great lie' picks up the untypical and makes it the cover all for failures. All earlier shortcomings were also not of the 'state apparatus', they were on account of 'feudal resistance', 'capitalistic carry-over', 'socialist revolution not yet complete' etc. How odd that I hear these phrases back home, too. There, as here, unquestioningly, unblinkingly all this is swallowed. That is why, the line which most frequently comes across on Afghanistan is: 'because Pakistan, supported by USA attacked Afghanistan'; or 'to help the poor people of Afghanistan.' And if you query about Poland it is: 'Solidarity is bad. It misleads workers to strike thus weakening socialism. It wishes to destroy communism'. Or, about travel: 'Why are you not able to go out when you want to and why do you not let people freely in?' 'Because there would be too much espionage.' But this last is different. This is demonstrative of xenophobia, about which some other time.

It is once again two in the morning and I am but a traveller.

In the nearby railway yard engines shunt and whistle evoking childhood nostalgia about trains forever moving. A little earlier, in the evening, just below my open window, in the apple orchard, a Kirghiz had strummed his mandolin and sung melodies as old as time, a time that had begun well before communism.

Still in Khirgizia

I DO NOT HAVE ANY INCLINATION OF GOING INTO A DETAILED description of this town itself; formerly 'Pish Peck', originally a fortress of the Kokand Khanate, lying on the 'Junction of three rivers: Ala Medin, Ala Archa and Chu', on the caravan route leading to the inner Tien Shan and China. In 1864, it became a part of the Russian Empire and that is when the very first of Russian settlers arrived in this Khirgiz town. For them (Europeans) it was the preferred destination—like our hill stations were for the Brits. To the nomadic Khirgiz, such settlements were an execration. To them the arrival of the Russians, replacing the Kokandi Khans of Uzbekistan made hardly any difference. (It does not cease to cause me wonderment that even late nineteenth century is here, in this town, considered 'ancient history'). Around 1878, it became a Czarist military garrison. At around the turn of that century the nomadic Khirgiz also began to settle down. The cataclysmic interventions of the First World War, the Great October Revolution, and to commemorate the memory of a young general of the Red Army: Mikhail Vasilivich Frunze (b: 1885 d: 1925), who died when only forty, this town of Pish Peck, his birthplace, got renamed as Frunze. (It would be interesting to investigate whether Gen. Frunze was purged? I am curious).

The landscape of Khirgizia

The Tien Shan, snow clad, form a great backdrop to this town, full of 'Europeanised parks;' laid by a Czarist officer Fetisov, in 1896. In the intervening period of almost a century these have now developed into impressive, cool, green back drops to the innumerable monuments that have since been erected to commemorate various heroes of the Revolution. '305 square metres of greenery to every citizen' is the kind of communist statistic that I am served and expected to then treasure. But Frunze is truly filled with very beautiful parks, very European monuments, the usual imposing buildings housing communist organs of state, and execrable, concrete, colonies for lodging human beings. 'We will raise them to fifteen storey buildings in the next five year plan!' I am informed by my diligent guide Sajida.

We were on this schizophrenic state of the Soviet mind when I, in fatigue, downed pen early this morning. It merits being summed up by a restatement. So conditioned is thinking that any deviation from it, or any questioning which attempts to break away these encrustations of falsehood, leads to a serious destabilisation. In any case, such a conditioning starts from childhood. By the time of adulthood or maturity, when an anchor of certainties, in the face of life's many travails has to be found this need too, is attempted to be met by the state. But communism, though attempting to be, is not religion, and it has neither the aura nor that subliminal 'belief in the irrational'. Its announced creed is the material plane. When therefore, deviations from mentally accepted thoughts are attempted, or when there is any destabilisation of the almost 'spiritual' moorings (in effect, at least), of the mind and belief of the citizenry of socialist states, then the very first is a violent and an almost hysterical disagreement. This is to be expected. Men and women do after all need to protect their beliefs as inviolate, they would otherwise flounder. But here lies the rub; if the system is built on the impossible presupposition of perfection ('I believe whatever the party does is right and in the interest of the Soviet people'—Sajida), then sooner or later will arrive that time when the sheer untenability of such incredible propositions will tear apart the very psyche of the 'believers'. If despite initial hysteric reactions we persist in our efforts at removing this 'encrustation' then we come to the 'phase of silence', as if the questioner were dim-witted, unable to grasp the obvious and a smile, privy as it were to some inner secret, replaces hysteria. Then there is circumlocution, answering my questions with counter queries, and finally, the ultimate of all weapons: 'You have been brainwashed by the Americans'.

It is similar when you discuss elections. A standard format seems to have been imparted to all. Invariably, therefore in 'capitalist societies' elections are 'corrupted by money'. You accept the presence of that evil but venture to suggest that possibly it is but a 'tiny fragment' of the entire. Of course, this is not believed, but when you query about 99.9% turnout, only one party, an 'official' list of candidates', or has anyone lost an election in the USSR etc., then a direct answer is evaded and a lengthy spiel follows on 'socialist democracy', the party is perfect etc. Where, one wonders, is there any place in such thinking for that kind of governance which 'is hardly observable when in use,'—or systems of such refinement.

My enquiry about 'millionaires' in Soviet Union from EU had resulted in a cynical and a rueful laugh from Sajida, it brought forth this astounding reply:

'There are no rich people in USSR. We only have official millionaires.' Now all this mind you, without a check, with no hesitation whatsoever and not the faintest sign of a blush at this absurd assertion.

'What is an official millionaire?' I had persisted. 'Oh! Poets, writers, heroes. They are permitted by state to keep money.' Time and again that nagging worry returns: Yes, the state does control all but who controls the state?

'And what do they do with their millions?'

'They lay them at the fount of Peace!'

That was a true winner. I was neatly floored. It was such a definitive, such a final piece of not just wool but really a great big pillow that the best I could do was to stay silent and try and escape asphyxiation.

'Do these heroes, poets etc. have children'?' I tried a different track.

'Yes, of course.'

'And what would happen to their money when these heroes etc. die.'

'They are not dead yet. They alive.'

'Yes. I am glad for them but when they eventually die, as we all must some day, what would happen to those millions?' So all pervading and so oppressive is this kind of mental conditioning that I felt nearly blasphemous uttering such irreverences as the possibility of mortal death for Soviet heroes. 'I not know.' This is the final barrier. This, and the 'It is not possible'. The latter is announced with predictable inevitability if you ask for a change in travel plans. The former, whenever one approaches the overload point. That is when the fuse of reasoning trips.

I had once enquired whether any development at all had taken place in Czarist Russia. 'No' was the firm and unequivocal reply. 'You

A busy Khirghizia market place

mean nothing at all?' Another 'No'. A bit riled by this refusal to see any but your own point as the right one, deliberately then I asked an absurd extension of the same question. (Now it is possible that that was not properly understood. However, despite that possibility the reply to it was staggering).

'Do you think life existed before the Great October Revolution?'

'No.'

'You mean nothing at all in the last fifty-nine thousand years or so of known Human History?'

'Oh,' giving an inch, 'some good things.'

I thought the affect would be spoilt if I enquired about details of those some 'good things'.

For example, in Frunze I inquired about a building, which stands square to the main administrative block: 'What is that?' That is the building of the Bureau of State Security! With such euphemisms I am only too familiar, but then deliberately, to provoke—'What is that? The army or the police?' I am met by a definitive silence. So patiently and one at a time but obstinately I persist.

'Well, what is it? 'State security', is it the responsibility of the Police?'

'No, it is not police.' Well, I am getting somewhere.

'Then it is the army?' so one would normally deduce.

'No, it is not the army.' I am not playing for a draw. I want check and mate.

'Then what is state security?'

'I do not know.' Stalemate. Inevitably, in time, regression from the original purity of the burning flame of revolution will take place.

It is discernible even now, and it is inevitable because of a fundamental dichotomy between socialist thought and socialist practice. To my mind such contradictions will increase. Those who are 'us' will continue to grow even richer, the existing disparities that will widen a new class of the rich is already there. These are the new 'haves' in a doctrinaire state, which is still but only theoretically of the 'have nots'. When that historical congruence of time and circumstance occurs, as it must, then the pendulum of change will oscillate in the reverse direction. Meanwhile, this vast state apparatus will continue to make itself more and more omnipotent and awe-inspiring.

This is nowhere as apparent as in the grand monuments and buildings that house the organs of state. Such monuments of awe-inspiring proportions dot all the cities. 'Heroes of the revolution', national poets, even chief of the first collective farm etc. They abound. They are necessary for domination. The physical proportion of such monuments is designed, with only that purpose in mind to over-awe. Hitler had them. So did all feudal monarchical orders. The state has to represent domination, power, therefore structures that house the organs of state (like the forts and palace of old must obviously be the most impressive. There may be housing shortages, as there are, and the houses for the citizenry may be of uniformly poor construction and depressingly drab in design, no matter. It is the organs of state that, must, (however wastefully) be housed in the most impressive and grandiose of structures. The rulers and the ruled must be distinctly apart. And of course the proletariat must know its place. One did not need a socialist revolution to arrive at that conclusion. Any defamed feudal of old could have told you that, though the king of Norway may ride a bicycle, or the prime minister of a capitalist democracy not infrequently walk to the House of the People, but not for the leaders of a Socialist state any such gesture, certainly not, not even symbolically.

10 August:

Until this morning I was the only tourist from foreign lands in this beautiful Czarist outpost of Khirgizia. Of course there were the 'recommended visitors' from friendly socialist countries like East Germany, Czechoslovakia, or Hungary and from the other Republics of USSR, but none from foreign lands. That was until this morning. I was then due to leave for a day in the country around Frunze and for a walk in the foothills of the Tien Shan.

I then found sitting alone in the bleak, deserted lobby of the hotel, a grey haired lady of some elegance, an island of gentility in this worker's haven. Her presence itself was an incongruity. She was still there when I returned from a walk in the foothills, and still sitting in the lobby as I returned from a walk around the park in the cool of the evening. I made enquiries and came to learn that she was from Turkey, and was here to visit some relative. That relative, too, I have seen, a rather decrepit and shabby looking individual—constantly under the influence of Vodka. All day long this sad, grey haired elegance has been in earnest conversation with her 'relative'. An incongruous string of pearls around her neck, in her dress and demeanour a refinement, in her hands a lace handkerchief, which she nervously twists and untwists, all the time whispering with such obvious intensity into the ears of her loutish relative. Who is she? And who is this her 'relative'? What compelling strands of emotion pull her to this far away Frunze from her native Turkey? What yawning gap of life is she attempting to fill by this visit now in the evening of her life? I embellish, no doubt, to what may perhaps be a perfectly straightforward situation, but all this could also almost be from Chekov!

Somehow, I had managed to extract permission to visit the countryside around Frunze and also the Tien Shan foothills. The Kirghiz, the Kazak and the Tatars are of Mongol descent, the Uzbek, the Tajik, the Turkmen all Indo-Semitic. But the Kirghiz are far less evident, in their own homeland, they have become a minority here.

Then those that are here have also almost completely been 'modernised'. The bazaar of Frunze bustles with activity but it lacks the colour, the originality and the native vitality of the bazaars of Uzbekistan. The Kirghiz, strangely for a horse-loving mountain people, are far less friendly. The Uzbek is volatile and extrovert, the Kirghiz proud, unsure and reserved behind his narrow, slit eyes. Possibly, this has something to do with them, as a tribe, straddling the Tien Shan mountains between USSR and China. There must be some spill-over to Hunza and possibly also in Afghanistan. I sense a deep insecurity amongst the Kirghiz here; what accounts for it? Not the dispute between USSR and China on this point, does it? When I enquire of this from Sajida, who is herself a Kirghiz, her reaction is needlessly animated: 'What you mean problem? You want Russia to give these mountains to China?' 'Of course, I do not, I only wanted to know.' As a nomadic people the Kirghiz have neither had any script nor any written history of their own. They do, have legends and a lifestyle that has evolved over the centuries, but none of the other outer manifestations of nationhood. They have wandered in these mountains for as long as memory serves, tending their sheep, cattle and horses, singing haunting melodies of the mountains and carrying massive eagles on their wrists far sport. Legend says there were forty sisters: 'Kirk-Ghiz', living in south Siberia. They all married, possibly one man, (poor wretch!) and moved to these mountains and sure enough a tribe was born. With 'forty' helping out it could not have been too difficult either. With such a history, total absorption by an expanding Soviet System could hardly be difficult, and yet I sense difficulties, though, I do not know what. I do know precisely, for example, that in no other Soviet Republic are there as many 'other nationalities' as here. There are even Germans from East Germany. It is wonderful to have all these statistics spouting out of a guide as bossy and diligent as Sajida but unfortunately, such numbers convey a lot and yet do not. The Khirgiz live their lifestyle, it survives, and these nomads continue to live largely as nomads.

The Ala Acha gorge is home for the nomads

We drove up the gorge of Ala Acha, with the magnificent Tien Shan as an imposing backdrop. Firs and conifer and juniper, though all much smaller in height dot the countryside, with private dachas all along the mountainous valleys—symbols of privilege and imperial occupation, (quite like the houses of the now departed British in our hill stations). A canal gurgles merrily down hill, running adjacent to the road. 'Water in this irrigation canal built by Soviet engineers travels at six meters per minute. Quite fast no?' I felt like answering. 'No', but thought better of it and instead I asked to be taken to a Kirghiz home. Sajida said 'No,' as of course. My driver Assad or Hasan, I never did quite establish which, was more enterprising. Though willing, unfortunately, his cooperative spirit was blunted by his lack of English, and by the presence of the formidable Sajida. They engaged in an argument. And while they were so involved, I asked to get out to take a photograph. Once outside, but without actually saying so in so many words I conveyed to Sajida that if 'she will not take me I will go on foot with Assad or Hasan'. That did it.

I am finally able to visit another private homestead with an orchard and a house—a proud Khirgiz grandmother, with great warmth invites me in (without shoes) and we sit on the ground whilst Sajida only initially though, in an assertion of her modernity advises me to sit on the only chair, The grandmother is not bothered with such peripherals, however. She fusses and brings out various items to eat—sour cream, butter, tea, bread, raspberry jam, raisins, all home made, and biscuits and toffee (state produce) as touches of modernity. She sits and watches me eat and complains that I did not give her any notice of my arrival otherwise she would have slaughtered a sheep! (Even sour and spinsterish Sajida softens— execrable alliteration that) And I could easily have been in a 'Bakarwal' or 'Gujar' (nomadic herdsmen) tent in Jammu, or with the 'Gaddis' in Himachal. We engage in a photography session thereafter with the granny posing with great seriousness.

At the end of this surprise meal, the grandmother had raised both her hands and praising Allah said 'Ameen'!

The kind and generous Grandmother who opened her home and her heart

Accompanied by Assad, I then went for a walk in the mountains. We could hardly converse but I kept him liberally supplied with Indian cigarettes and kept repeating 'Kirghiz tent'—'Horses'. He took me to both, this enterprising Assad. And there I 'distributed food to the natives', took photographs and drank 'kumis' (fermented mare's milk—not bad at all, if you can hold your breath, that is, while drinking!)

The landmass of the USSR is one-sixth of the total landmass on the surface of the earth. Add to it the cushions of friendly Socialist countries in East Europe, Finland, neutralised Scandinavia, and the enormous Central Asian land spaces of Mongolia and you have a modern state of staggering proportions. It is the only country that touches three oceans. Its depth of land is enormous. Its existing and potential economic might can be geared for instant mobilisation.

Food is not in surplus, its shortage always a fearsome possibility, thus a sharing of it seems to be expected. I gave the charwomen in the hotel my unused boiled eggs. This made her ecstatic, she even managed a grimace of a smile and that is 'ecstasy' coming from these uniformly grim and unsmiling hotel attendants. Incidentally, I have discovered that a boiled egg is perhaps the only dish that is cooked in an edible manner in these parts.

An auxiliary and a reserve of the Soviet fleet, the vast aircraft fleet of Aeroflot dovetailed with Soviet Air Force, the state militia and the young pioneers and Comsoms, all reserves. This plus the space programme and the nuclear missiles all cost money. But then the economies of the East European states are to subserve, before any other requirement, the needs and demands of Moscow. These state economies and the state apparatuses of those countries are primarily to serve the interests of the USSR. Poland is seriously, and for the first time, questioning all this and fearfully, one wonders for how long before the denouement.

The Soviet Union is the mightiest imperial power of this century. It has a highly centralised and xenophobic state apparatus. The actions of its leaders do not have to face the glare of any public scrutiny. And as a state, it is not enfeebled by any doubting morality, questioning liberals or such ethical dilemmas as the question of means and ends. In its 'internal' management, it has long since abandoned any questioning of means. It carries no inhibitions on that score, no matter what its pretensions to the contrary. The very creation of this mighty state apparatus and a mighty military machine has generated its own impulse, creating a vast, ever expanding movement which can keep expanding but only till the life of this 'movement' lasts; when that impulse begins to weaken, then what? And when will that be? and what then will happen? Will this cosmos implode? Who knows?

Such is the reality of twentieth century Russia. In India, we are directly and vitally affected. In this grand design of Russian expansionism, we are already a dependency for military hardware and for almost forty percent of our export trade. Successive governments in Delhi have sown the seeds of this potentially difficult situation. As signatories to a treaty of peace and friendship and belonging as we do to that club, we have willingly undertaken to articulate the strategic perceptions of this mighty twentieth century Imperial power. Finally, in its ever expanding process of assimilation, suction of the smaller neighbours, assertion of the zone of influence, USSR has undertaken the most decisive imperial step in Asia, in recent history. Its occupation of Afghanistan. This will have incalculable consequences. It is time for us in India to sit up and recognise that reality.

It is time to leave, to strike camp, distant pastures summon. How distant already feels the Central Asian Kirghiz town of Frunze, as I prepare to leave for Irkutsk and Siberia and Mongolia tomorrow. And then China. 'Siberia'.... Cheerful thought.

Leave Taking

Notes from my Diary

Day of sightseeing before leaving for Irkntsk in Siberia

—Late arrival, rather no car—my cold anger—Sajida 'Chief has taken car' 'Why?' 'Meeting Central Committee.'

'What about the money that I have paid?'

'I am sorry cannot criticise Chief' 'Why not'?' and more in that vein. Ride in a Soviet bus!

Museum of Fine Arts 'Revolutionary art, people's artist, people's Sculptor. On the depiction of a Siberia returned czarist prisoner —'You have prisoners in Siberia even now'—'No, we do not, we keep them there.' 'Ah so you have crime in USSR?' (emphatically) —— 'No', Then whom do you keep in prisons?' 'That people who not get along in society'; Later 'This is revolutionary art we have much progress in this department.' 'You Kirghiz use Russian script?' 'Yes.' 'Why not Arabic?' 'We find very difficult. It imperial and feudal' 'And Russian' 'We proud, proud to use Russian.'

At Memorial to Frunze: 'Was he a Russian?' 'No a Moldavian'— 'But still a European?' 'He was a revolutionary Hero of the Great Revolutionary war. He liberated Central Asia from White Russian Army' 'What was that?' 'All foreigners and capitalists and some rich people from here who did not like the poor.'

In the Exhibition an achievement, I am swamped by stastics—267 varieties of roses, three hundred thousand streams and rivers, three thousand lakes (she had made notes on a tissue paper)—mind boggling and excruciatingly boring.

I feel suffocated, imprisoned and struggling to escape from this all pervading lie, this paralysing hypocrisy. What have human beings done to humans? Endless delays with car—Assad driving like a fiend.

Siberia

Irkutsk

It had rained in Frunze by the time it came for me to leave. The atmosphere had turned soft and the temperature was lower. I will always remember Frunze, for various things—its beauty and its air and its water—the people, but also the terrible muddle with my programmes that Intourist got me into. The departure was typical. No car. Then fiendish driving by Assad, the airport being about forty minutes drive away from the hills.

Soon after leaving Frunze, the Central Asian steppes begin and the horizon becomes one unbroken line. In that soft, rain washed atmosphere, as we drove, upon my consciousness got imprinted tiny vignettes, they stay on my mind as eradicable pictures: A woman with an umbrella walking through the fields her skirt billowing in the breeze; cows and white geese herded by a young girl with a birch twig in her hand, the cows placid and ruminant, the geese waddling and quacking self importantly; two boys riding a bicycle over a bridge shouting—(I think)—forbidden obscenities as boys would; the sun setting in the western horizon and suddenly multiple rainbows; the Tien Shan behind us still enveloped in dark, cumulonimbus clouds;

droves and droves of swallows circling and swooping and chattering in the soft evening air; an ineffable peace, a sense of this land having gone on and on and on forever—these wide immeasurably open steppes with gently waving grass, fragrant and rain washed—miles upon thousands of miles of it, beyond the reach of human eye. Here before we came, and here still long after we leave.

The plane is full of Russian Muzhiks, for it is to Siberia that we are going. A plane full of peasants with bundles of unmanageable handbags and those interminable pieces of paper—little tokens of legitimacy—clutched fearfully in sweating palms. Yelling, crying children. Some geese and chicken in baskets would complete the scene like in a Hogarth painting. The inside of the aircraft turns hot and foetid. As soon as the passengers are seated, bundles are opened and boiled potatoes and overripe apples and pickled gherkins emerge, to be chewed on with single-minded stolidity. The air gets filled with an indiscriminate mixture of so many food baskets, perspiring humanity, and the sharp rancid stench of nappies being changed. It is all indescribably beautifully alive and vital, like our village fairs, or our railway platforms, where life flows, lived continuously, constantly, uninhibitedly, with both unconcern and with fatalism. So it is in this Russian aircraft—particularly fatalism.

By the time the aircraft lifts off, it is a half past nine at night. The eastern horizon is dark and a three-quarter moon slowly emerges as if being pulled up. In the west though, it is still light. There is a strange sensation of suspension, between day and night, of being almost disembodied. The aircraft labours to gain height, weighed and heavy, therefore struggling to ascend. We bank and turn north-north east. Slowly night spreads all around, seeming to swallow this winged insect of a craft: for we are heading directly into night because of which, below us, not a speck of light, not one can be seen, just dark, blank, virgin earth. Then not slowly, not gradually but with a suddenness that is unnerving, a storm of fearsome, primeval energy develops. And, it is sudden for we have flown into it. The sky is suddenly ablaze, lit by fearsome lightning, of such intensity as I do not remember when I last witnessed. Great bolts of Jehova tear the night sky apart, sheets upon sheets of them assailing the earth and the atmosphere; every ticking of the second on the watch hand is filled with many multiple numbers of them. I am filled with awe and so fascinated as to hardly notice the buffeting our frail craft is getting (with predictable consequences, of course). Riveted to the window, I watch. The aeroplane banks and circles and wants to get around the storm. But the dimension of it, the sheer physical measure of it is such as can only be described in superlatives—it takes us over an hour of jet flying speed just to go round. I lose a sense of time, but do know that in such a storm any attempt to fly through it would have been suicidal.

Slowly the lightning begins to get left behind; we are escaping the clutches of the storm, but its ferocity is still unabated. By now the moon is high, and there below us lies the Earth so much darker. Then slowly spreads below, a soft carpet of white clouds and in the pale glow of the moon this cloud cover turns ephemeral, like an endless stretch of snow, with drifts and eddies and crevasses wherever cloud banks cast deep shadows but always as soft as fleece and as bewitching as a lullaby. From the ineffable peace of the evening just before leaving Frunze to this elemental storm (over the Siberian steppes) and now, back again to this indescribably peaceful and tranquil outside—the effect of all this on my mind is as if this had all been arranged for me. Words fail to do any justice to what I have just experienced. It was Siberian in all its dimensions, like a celestial symphonic poem—the music of the very heavens themselves, on a scale and with a harmony that no human hand can ever devise.

Notes from my Diary

— The view of a forest fire in the blank darkness below—Vivid glow—two moons? One in the heavens—another on Earth.

— Smoking in the aircraft lavatory with a Russian peasant travelling to Khabravosk, no language—plenty of communication—no one bothers about fire or security

The moon slides down the sky; we are aiding it in its descent now by winging away from it in our fragile cocoon, this tiny flying machine. Again, mile upon mile, endless half-hours of not even a speck of light anywhere below. The first sign of an approaching Irkutsk is just a pinpoint of a light in this gloom below.

We taxi to an empty airport building. Figures outside wearing overcoats. No Intourist reception, yet again. An Aeroflot girl walks me from one end of the empty airport building to another—'Wait here'. After sometime—'Come with me'—another room, 'Wait here'. Curiously, I remain placid. Then 'For tonight you go to a transit hotel, tomorrow Intourist' I reply 'Nyet', but I am smiling. 'You no go?' 'No'. She does not even argue. I have no intentions of sharing a dormitory with fifteen other rude and snoring members of the proletariat, not after the great high of experience that I had just been through, that wonder of a flight. Workers of the world ought certainly to unite, but elsewhere and at some other time and with someone else. There is a piano in the lounge; tunelessly I strum its keys in an empty, echoing hall.

Finally, a taxi arrives. I refuse to pay for it, demanding payment by Intourist. The girl by now knows. She advises a reluctant and surly driver accordingly. Cabbies are the same the world over. This is my first taxi ride in USSR. It is half past four of a cool Siberian morning. Empty streets glistening in the light of street lamps, the cabbie styles himself on those of the New York variety and has a cigarette dropping from one corner of his mouth. He spoils it by having hair like the Beatles. He ruins it further and finally, by condescending to acknowledge my thanks with the faintest suggestion of a smile.

I arrive to a 'people-less' hotel. The only sign of life is a fussy, bespectacled young man who rushes out in nervous panic.

'Good afternoon! Mr. Singh, so sorry you had to wait at the airport.' It is five in the morning!

'Good afternoon!' I reply.

A girl is woken up to register me. She hands 'Grisha' (for that is 'good afternoon's' name) a message.

'Mr. Singh your train reservation is booked from Ulan Bator to Peking on the 16th'—in a peculiarly Russian way (which to me is the final romantic touch), on a dark dawn, in a silent and sleepy hotel in Siberia to be informed that my train passage through the Gobi desert is booked for a date that lies in the future.*

---

*   My travels after Siberia had taken me through the Gobi desert, then to the People's Republic of China entering at Erlian, thence to Beijing and Shanghai and much else. But that was a different journey that travel went well beyond Transoxiana.

Irkutsk

'Sit down before you go'

Notes from my Diary

1. Lake Baikal
At Irkutsk girl fishing in Lake Baikal
- 30,000 sq.km
- 300 rivers fall into it
- Only one goes out "Angara"
- Max depth: 1643 meters; Fish at that depth
- 22% of the world's fresh water
- supply-80% of USSR
Siberia ————10 million sq.km
Virgin Taiga—7.8 million sq.km (78%)
Another view of Lake Baikal
2. The autonomous Republic of Buryat
- Capital : Ulan Ude
- 50% Buddhists & 50% Christians
- The tree strung with cloth pieces enroute to Lake Baikal
- Ulan: Red/Great/Beautiful

- Ude: mountain
- Must learn more about the Buriyats who I think, are on the verge of extinction. I hope not. A gentle, mild, Buddhist Island in the midst of atheist materialism—why declined?

The Russians say that before you embark on a journey, sit down. It is a metaphorical 'looking back', a stock taking, a collection of your energies. That at least is the interpretation that I give to it. Unavoidably, then my journal too, of *Travels in Transoxiana*, must sit down in Siberia, before it leaves.

This Russian North, and East, is an incomparable land. How appropriate to sit down here, therefore, and reflect a bit. One gets cautious of the superlatives that have to be used when describing it or its people, but there is no other way. As for my travels, except perhaps, for the terrible loneliness of Tashkent and the strange and unbearable feeling of captivity in Frunze, I have been enthralled by all that I have seen and experienced. These heroic people, stoically living with a system that is inhumanity personified. Of course the people are not charming; they are 'elemental'—and in that, too, lies their attraction for me: Unrefined, coarse, brutal, uncompromising but...human.

Lake Baikal

Last night I broke my fortnight's fast and had Vodka and wine (the full works) with dinner. The effort was pathetic. Alcohol brought no relief. Not even that of the absolution of inebriation.

After a while one stops persisting. So in the cool and soft light of an early Siberian evening, I went for a long walk along the Angara River—bustling, busy and choked to near fullness with tugs and river vessels of all kinds. A luminous sky, the moon now hanging over the railway yard, and on the city across the other bank.

The Irkutsk railway yard is bustling permanently with activity. It is 'The' central station of the Trans-Siberia railway route; freight trains a full kilometer long—and trains swinging to Peking; South and onwards, to the Pacific coast. The romance of railway yards in a strange city, in far away lands, with trains always leaving. Also distant trains, whistling long signals of arrival, from far away and yet arriving only to leave again.

I walked and sat on a bench, for there was no sleep in my eyes. Fatigue had broken that barrier, which after being breached, the body and the consciousness just keep moving and all the while fatigue is left just that far behind, just behind the eyelids, but unable to catch up and force them shut. This Siberian evening turned into night, full of a round moon high in the sky now, and of the romance of troikas and Russian winters, and the trembling, shivering passions of the tragic Anna Karenina; the music of this land; also the land of 'Shamans!' (We were on the shores of the Baikal just where the Angara parts company with the lake. An island in the middle of the rapids is called the 'Shaman' Island. 'Why?' I had asked. 'For on it a man who could tell the future used to sit.' Soon thereafter, a Russian police man walked by carrying a 'walkie talkie'. 'There goes a Shaman', Vitali with Latin quick-silverness had quipped). This land of wandering minstrels, and the black nights of winter in the Taiga, of dark inscrutable magic and sooth sayers and fortune tellers and so much else.

Uzbekistan was full of wonder, history, the romance of the past and a colourful present. Khirghizia filled me strangely with forebodings, of latent violence and oppression, and this Russian North and East is such a revelation. I have to visit again. It is, to me, pure and glitteringly, uncompromisingly, passionately, Russian.

So after a while I got up from the bench and walked along the by now silent streets of this town. I walked as fancy took me. The town was dark and silent. I had been so foolish as to leave the hotel

Old Irkutsk

A church in old Irkutsk

in merely a shirt. It became cold. There is, under the best of circumstances, not much traffic in Siberian outposts. By now, therefore, the streets were empty and but for prowling cats and some drunken sailors or soldiers, I encountered nobody. But now I was keen to return; also beginning to get desperate because I could not find my way. There was no one to ask directions from. I began to feel the cold—shivering, and my sandaled (Central Asian) feet felt frozen. I knew I had to only find the riverbank and all would then be well. But where was the riverbank?

Irkutsk is wholly Russian, at least what I have always imagined Russia to be. There is no impression here of it being part of any empire, like with the Uzbek or the Kirghiz. Here, only the Buryat stand, in silent and withdrawn aggrievement, a Buddhist island of peaceful resignation. How far these ideas of the great Buddha carried, for while the Buryat, a gentle, docile people unassertively live in 'settlement', Ulan Ude becomes 'half Chistian'! Yet, in the tying shreds of cloth to trees by citizens is a symbolic and a living affirmation of continuity. I draw hope even from that gesture.

In 1879 Irkutsk had burnt down. I was in search of that old Irkutsk. Russian orthodox churches and old wooden houses, the 'incomparable faces' of the Russian East. I could just not be content with blazingly modern sports stadia and monuments of heroes of the revolution and such others. I was not interested in what the mighty apparatus of the state had put up as symbols of power of grandeur or whatever. I wanted to witness the results of the flowering of the peoples of this land. Once again it was the driver who gave in first. Vitali showed me an Irkutsk, which would take a whole history to describe.

—In the background, three churches. In the fore, young soldiers touting stenguns or their Russian equivalents, at the ready.

—Two hoboes whom I badly want to photograph. 'Can I?' 'They will beat you with their broom if you try'—'Let us anyway'—so I put the guide as a pretence in the foreground.

—An old woman; 'go and ask if I may photograph her.' The guide does so. The woman replies: 'I am not feeling well'. Shamelessly, I go ahead any way.

It is time, anyway, to leave for Mongolia, the Gobi and then China.

Because, it was Mongolia that had given birth to this great nomadic civilisation, that swept all, conquered nearly the whole of the Asian/European landmass, knocked on the gates of Christendom and subjugated Hungary. It penetrated southwards to China, to Persia in the West, and left dynamic progeny in Uzbekistan: Taimur, Ulugh Beg, Babur (of the Mongol Barlos tribe) who eventually carried the sword of Islam into India. This was the fount-head. What impulsion was it that propelled them and why did it dry up? It is with these questions I had undertaken *Travels in Transoxiana*.

An aside on the causes of decline of Buddhism whether in Mongolia or elsewhere. It (Buddhism) became effete; the Lamas, in any case, led introverted lives, remote from the people; used Tibetan language in texts and while preaching and thus removed themselves from their own followers. Secondly, unlike Christianity for example, Buddhism did not modernise itself and was thus unable to cope with the change, more so scientific change. It failed to comprehend the challenge of 'dialecticism', leave alone lead any resistance to it. I add another reason, for to my mind, it was also because that original fount of thought, India, had itself lost its vitality and conviction. Thereafter, the dictatorial Lamas practised, and not just simply preached but actually insisted upon celibacy.

The population rapidly declined, inevitably. It was 6,70,000 when the Revolution came.

The strength of this great nomadic civilisation and its vigour lay in their unceasing quest for ever new pastures. This meant movement and even though the lands were vast, movement brought in its wake conflict, a fight over pastures. But here, combined with great physical hardihood was the immeasurably strengthening factor of there being nothing to lose! Defeat meant merely a search for yet another pasture, and possibly yet another conflict. Plus, there was the horse. It was, or must have been in its time, as revolutionary a vehicle of carriage and offence as was the tank in this century. The massed effect of Mongol cavalry can only be conjectured now, but it could not have been anything short of paralysing. Inevitably therefore, conquests came. It was from this fountain of vigour that Babur, too, emerged; a Mongol of the Barlos tribe; a descendant of Temugin (Chengej) and Taimur.

The roots lie here. Not very original, perhaps, but I am able to 'sense', only just sense, though not yet fully comprehend this great sweep, a certain historical inevitability. What a phenomenal circle of events it becomes—Babur travels along the old silk route to establish an Islamic kingdom in India. But in his homeland, from the land of his conquests arrives in the form of Buddhist thought, not the sword, not death but through the high plateaus of Tibet, and the Aksai Chin, the Takla Makan and the mighty deserts of Mongolia, this faith of Buddhism. These great movements of thoughts and events have occurred in the past and will surely continue for as long as humanity survives.

Why then did the 'impulse' lose its dynamism? The moment nomads became static and acquired the characteristics of the conquered, those very characteristics which in the first instance had led to the defeat of the settled, static communities, then the vigour of the nomad had also to dissolve in time. Besides, these conquering nomadic civilisations had little administrative sense. They were a sweeping force, but the strengths of the settled civilisations quickly assimilated them. When, therefore the 'nomadic herdsmen' became 'the Khans', then that burning flame of their great energy also got dimmed at first, then finally extinguished. Islam, when it replaced the Shamanism of the graziers, imparted fresh energy, but in time that too wilted. So much was given by Islam—it took back very little. But it had been a great run after all.

Travels in Transoxiana was an inner search, an outer exploration, a quest for roots and for some guiding beacons, for the future. I found a great deal, but there is so much left to be found still.

Campfires go down, the first cold kiss of autumn touches the Siberian Taiga. It is time for the Kafila (the caravans) to leave; to move, and then to return some other summer, to these bountiful pastures again.

> As firmly cemented clam-shells
> Fall apart in autumn,
> So I must take to the road again.

(AN INCOMPLETE HAIKU BY BASHA—AD 1676)